T0209158

SECRETS OF SUCCESSFUL
WEALTHY ENTREPRENEURS

Become a Successful Wealthy Entrepreneur in a Dynamic, Complex and Volatile Environment

Kingstone P. Ngwira

authorHOUSE®

AuthorHouse™
1663 Liberty Drive
Bloomington, IN 47403
www.authorhouse.com
Phone: 833-262-8899

Published by AuthorHouse 09/23/2020

ISBN: 978-1-6655-0133-0 (sc)
ISBN: 978-1-6655-0131-6 (hc)
ISBN: 978-1-6655-0132-3 (e)

Library of Congress Control Number: 2020918609

Print information available on the last page.

This book is printed on acid-free paper.

Scripture quotations taken from the Holy Bible, King James Version
(Authorized Version). First published in 1611. Quoted from the KJV Classic
Reference Bible, Copyright © 1983 by The Zondervan Corporation.

Contents

Dedication vii

Acknowledgements... ix

Preface xi

Introduction.. xiii

Part I: Nature of Entrepreneurship

Chapter 1   Successful Wealthy Entrepreneurs: Angels of
             Economic Growth 1
Chapter 2   Capture Business Opportunities 7
Chapter 3   Start With What You Have................................. 24
Chapter 4   Develop a Great Product or Service................... 29
Chapter 5   Understanding Markets 31
Chapter 6   Attract and Retain High Performing People in
             your Business.. 37
Chapter 7   Location and Facilities Layout 42
Chapter 8   Financing the Business..................................... 47
Chapter 9   Understanding Legal Environment of Business............. 50

Part II: Crave for Principles of Success

Chapter 10   Take Business as a Calling 74
Chapter 11   Craft Clear Strategic Vision 76
Chapter 12   Plan for Success 79
Chapter 13   Understanding Business Ethics 83
Chapter 14   Let the Figures Make Noise 91
Chapter 15   Improve on Stakeholder Management Skills 94

Chapter 16   Create a Winning Recipe 102

Chapter 17   Business on Shoestring 107

Chapter 18   Never Give Up But Work Hard, Hard, Hard 112

Part III: Starting and Growing A Great Successful Business

Chapter 19   Creativity, Invention and Innovation 124

Chapter 20   Getting Started 129

Chapter 21   Develop a Successful Business Plan 142

Chapter 22   Venture Growth Stages 148

Chapter 23   Competitive Advantage Issues 152

Part IV: Mastering Wealthy Creation Principles

Chapter 24   How to Become and Stay Wealthy 160

Chapter 25   The Importance of Entrepreneurs to Wealth Creation ... 165

Chapter 26   Things You Did Not Know About Successful
             Wealthy Entrepreneurs 169

Chapter 27   Mastering the Business Model: Revenue, Profits
             and Costs 174

Part V: Harvesting A Dog Business

Chapter 28   Retrenchment 188

Chapter 29   Divestment 191

Chapter 30   Succession Planning 194

Conclusion 199

References 201

Dedication

To all Entrepreneurs who aspire to become wealthy like me.

To my family and friends who have supported me from day one.

Special dedication to my wife, Shannila whose unconditional love cannot go without annotation.

To my sons, Pastor Prince and Gift, you are my greatest inspiration to achieve my strategic vision. God will reward you for standing with me all the times. Thank you for supporting me on my path to success and comforting me during challenging times.

Acknowledgements

To Start with, I want to acknowledge the wonders of God upon my life are because of the King of Kings. There is no one like Him and He does what He says He will do. Thank you, Lord, for transforming my life and raising me as one of the successful wealthy Entrepreneurs in my generation.

This book has taken more than five (5) years of preparation and has been written in (3) three years. Hence the obvious impact that it will bring upon your life as a reader.

To all the members of Staff at Great Dominion Holdings Limited (GDHL) in Lilongwe, Malawi. Thank you for creating room for me to share and test these developed concepts with you.

Preface

In one of my books entitled, "The Road to Entrepreneurship," I said, "If you dedicate yourself to applying the strategies presented in this book, you will become wealthy. And if you make this book part of your life, it will make you rich." The same statement goes out to you as you read this life transforming book. If you apply the secrets presented in this book, which are a function of studying how successful wealthy Entrepreneurs become wealthy, this book will make you become a wealthy Entrepreneur.

My dear reader, I have repeated the aforementioned statement with complete confidence because this book consists of tested and proven principles. The book brings to you practical, proven instructions from people who have actually accomplished great strides in the field of entrepreneurship.

Entrepreneurship represents a vital source of change in all facets of society, empowering individuals to seek opportunities where others see insurmountable problems. Technologicaly entrepreneurship as a style of business leadership involves identifying highly-potential, technology-intensive commercial opportunities, gathering resources such as talent and capital, and managing rapid growth and significant risks using principled decision-making skills.

Early in my career, it became obvious to me that education gives you a big edge in business. Risk, which is always a part of doing business, is substantially reduced when you learn everything you can about what you are getting into. People who are more educatedand prepared even beyond formal education have an entrepreneurship advantage. That is what has greatly contributed to my success.

The purpose of this book is targeting two types of people. First, those that aspire to become successful Wealthy Entrepreneurs like me, even though they have not started any venture at all. Secondly, those that are in business but are unsuccessful entrepreneurs and have failed to achieve a desire to become successful wealthy Entrepreneurs. I have the overwhelming confidence and beliefs that both billionaire entrepreneurs and corporate workers (Intrapreneurs) will get something from this book. I also believe that anyone who has a failed business venture will read this book and learn the secrets which will help avoid pitfalls in future.

If only you can focus on implementing the secrets presented in this book in the next 90 days, I can guarantee you that you will be on the path to become wealthy no matter who you are and where you are now. Most people never take the time to come up with even a basic plan for building wealth and becoming financially empowered and secure. By learning from the experts in this book, you are way ahead of the game. I therefore, encourage you to read this book but more importantly, go and practice them!

Kingstone P. Ngwira

Introduction

I wished I knew then what I know now. It goes without saying that if you do what successful people do, there is a high probability that you can also become successful. This is the reason why I want to thank you for deciding to read this book. In the pages that follows, you are going to learn the secrets that will make you become a successful wealthy entrepreneur. Whenever the principles and concepts presented in this book will be applied, you will become a successful wealthy Entrepreneur.

Many business commentators say that the green shoots of entrepreneurship give an economy its vitality. They give rise to new products and services, fresh applications for existing products and services, and new ways of doing business. Entrepreneurship stirs up the existing economic order and prunes out the dead wood. Established companies that fail to adapt to the changes cease to be competitive in the marketplace and go out of business.

Within the broadest definition, entrepreneurs are found throughout the world of business because any firm, big or small, must have its share of entrepreneurial drive if it is to survive and prosper.

This book is written from three sources: first, accessed knowledge from my mentors on entrepreneurship; second, are courses which I have taught in Universities both local and international as a Professor of Business and Management Studies, and above all, my own entrepreneurial experience in my own entrepreneurial ventures.

I would like to emphasize the purpose of this book with joy that while this book is going to empower would-be Entrepreneurs to start and grow their new business ventures and become successful wealthy entrepreneurs, it is not only for them. The book is also for those that are already in business but are struggling. They will learn transforming secrets about entrepreneurship, crave for success, learn skills that are required to start and grow a successful business, master wealth creation principles and also learn the principles of harvesting in business that include: retrenchment strategy; divestment and succession planning.

PART I

NATURE OF ENTREPRENEURSHIP

CHAPTER 1

Successful Wealthy Entrepreneurs: Angels of Economic Growth

Who is an entrepreneur?

An **Entrepreneur** is one who creates a new business in the face of risk and uncertainty for the purpose of achieving profit and growth by identifying opportunities and assembling the necessary resources to capitalize on those opportunities. **Entrepreneurs usually start with nothing more than an idea – often a simple one – and then organize the resources necessary to transform that idea into a sustainable business.** One business writer defined an Entrepreneur as "Someone who takes nothing for granted, assumes change is possible and follows through, someone incapable of confronting reality without thinking about ways to improve it and for whom action is a natural consequence of thought."

Many people dream of owning their businesses and become wealthy but most of them never launch the business or company. Those who take an entrepreneurial plunge will experience the thrill of creating something grand from nothing; they will also discover the challenges and difficulties of building a business "from scratch". Whatever their reasons for choosing entrepreneurship, satisfaction only comes from running their own businesses the way they choose.

Researchers have invested a great deal of time and effort over the last decade studying Entrepreneurs and trying to paint a clear picture of the "entrepreneurial personality." Although these studies have produced several characteristics Entrepreneurs tend to exhibit, none of them has isolated a set of traits required for success.

Table 1: Summary of Entrepreneurial Profile

1	Desire for responsibility
2	Preference for moderate risk
3	Confidence in their ability to succeed
4	Desire for immediate feedback
5	High level of energy
6	Future orientation
7	Skill at organizing
8	Value of achievement over money
9	High degree of commitment
10	Tolerance of ambiguity
11	Flexibility
12	Tenacity

Entrepreneurs have many of the same character traits as Leaders. However, Trait-based theories of entrepreneurship are increasingly being called into question.

Entrepreneurship is at times being questionably associated with managers and administrators who are said to be more methodical and less prone to risk- taking. Such person centric models of entrepreneurship have shown questionable validity. Many real-life Entrepreneurs operate in teams rather than as single individuals.

Four Types of Entrepreneurs

1. Innovators
2. The Calculating Inventor
3. The Over Optimistic Promoter,
4. The Organization Builder.

These types are not related to personalities but to the type of opportunity the Entrepreneur faces. Robinson (2010) mentions that, for the Entrepreneur to succeed, he or she needs to cultivate the following attribute: The Entrepreneur should have an enthusiastic vision which is the driving force of an enterprise. This entrepreneur's vision is usually supported by an interlocked collection of specific ideas not available at the market place. The overall blue print to realize this vision is clear, however details may be incomplete, flexible and involving.

An Entrepreneur promotes the vision with enthusiastic passion; with persistence and determination. Entrepreneurs develop strategies to change the vision into reality. They take the initial responsibility to cause a vision to become a success by taking prudent risks. They asses cost, market/ customer needs and persuade others to join and help; and are usually positive thinkers and decision makers.

Development of Entrepreneurship

The understanding of entrepreneurship owes much to the work of economist Joseph Schumpeter and the Austrian economists such as Ludwig von Mises and von Hayek. **Schumpeter (1961) states that an entrepreneur is a person who is willing and able to convert a new idea or invention into successful innovations.**

Entrepreneurship forces "creative destruction" in a way that creative destruction is largely responsible for the dynamism of industries and long- run economic growth. Despite Schumpeter's early 20th century contributions, the traditional microeconomic growth of economies has had little room of Entrepreneurs in its theoretical frameworks. Much of the literature on entrepreneurship can be divided into broad camps focus on individuals and structure respectively (Peters 1998).

They first seek to explain the prevalence of Entrepreneurs in terms of innate psychological traits or how special characteristics are formed in certain social groups. The second highlights how social cultural structures call forth Entrepreneurs by providing opportunities for entrepreneurship.

The goal is not always to explain entrepreneurial action on micro level, but rather the amount of entrepreneurial activity in a certain place or time (Radebaugh 2005).

An early and important contribution to the study of entrepreneurial individuals was David McClelland's the Achievement society '(1961).

3

McClelland argued that some societies have cultural attitudes, which translate into primary socialization practices that foster entrepreneurial individuals. Nickels et al (2005) similarly argued that the entrepreneurial personality was the result of a particularly painful upbringing.Other researchers have sought the entrepreneurial personality in risk-taking propensity, internal locus of control, tolerance for ambiguity: over-optimism and need for autonomy (Stevenson 2005).

The structural tradition on the other hand seeks to understand how social, cultural and institution factors induce entrepreneurship. Some argued that deviance and marginality encourage entrepreneurship, but most authors instead emphasizes that cultural and institutional support, including good access to resources, is what encourages entrepreneurship (Sullivan 2001).

Nickels et al (2005) break this down in regulatory terms (e.g. institutions and policies), and cognitive factors (e.g. knowledge on how to start ventures and obtain financial support), and normative factors (e.g. the perception of entrepreneurship as career), which are used to explain both types and levels of entrepreneurship in different countries. Management researchers often emphasize the special influence of organizations and especially prior employment in established firms (Hisrich 1998).

Organizations are said to serve three critical functions: they provide opportunities and build confidence especially in the ability to create a new organization; provide general industry knowledge about entrepreneurial opportunities; and provide social networks and access to critical resources (Daniel 2004). As mentioned, these approaches typically seek to explain the amount of entrepreneurial activity.

Criticism

The Traditional approach has been criticized for failing to account for entrepreneurial action on the micro level.

The Individual's approach has been criticized for its single-cause logic, insensitivity to temporal dynamics and failure to account for contextual factors. The Situational approach is criticized for its focus on adaptation and consequently failure to account for human agency.

The current trend is instead to regard heterogeneity in terms of knowledge, preferences, abilities, behaviors etc. as a fundamental assumption for theory building (Nickels at al 2005). The increased focus on heterogeneity naturally downplays interest in stable personality traits and broad contextual pressures in favor of more detailed investigations and explanations of entrepreneurial action.

Entrepreneurship in the 21st Century

This is an Entrepreneur age. Entrepreneurship is often perceived as a difficult undertaking, as vast majorities of new businesses fail. Entrepreneurial activities are substantially different depending on the type of organization that is being started. Entrepreneurship ranges in scale from solo projects also known as swivivalsts (individualism) to major projects undertaking many job opportunities.

Entrepreneurship is the sense of free enterprise because the birth of new business gives a market economy its vitality. Many business commentators say that the Entrepreneur is a person of very high aptitude who pioneers change, processing characteristics found in only a very small fraction of the population. On the other hand of definitions, anyone who wants to work for himself is considered to be an Entrepreneur.

Peters (2012) supports the above views and states that entrepreneurship results in creation, enhancement, realization of value, not just for owners, for all participants and stakeholders. At the heart of this process is the creation and or recognition of opportunities followed by the will and initiative to seize these opportunities. It requires willingness to take risks, both personal and financial- but in a very calculated fashion in order to constantly shift the odds to your favorable balancing the risks with potential reward.

Many writers share the above views and comment that Entrepreneurs devise ingenious strategies to marshal their limited resources. This means that they are people who see opportunities where others see chaos. They move into an area and start making money while others wonder-what are these people doing in this dry and dead place.

Economic Prospective Entrepreneurial on Action

Schumpeter is arguably the most influential economist of entrepreneurship. In Schumpeter's writing, the individual Entrepreneur embodies the innovation function in society and stands out as a leader in an otherwise equilibrating world of habitant actors. Contrary to the rest of the population, Entrepreneurs are creative actors who are defined by their non-rational extraordinary qualities.

Schumpeter saw information as having any unique knowledge or capabilities compared to non- Entrepreneurs. Schumpeter rather emphasized the non-utilitarian qualities of Entrepreneurs speculated about their unique psychological make-up. Schumpeter also stressed the practical side of entrepreneurship, arguing that Entrepreneurs are individuals that 'get things done' in society.

CHAPTER 2

Capture Business Opportunities

Often the most attractive opportunity for many people is that of owning and managing their own businesses. Millions of people from all over the world have taken an entrepreneurial challenge and succeeded. Tremendous opportunities exist for all men and women willing to take the risk of starting a business

Start Up Business Opportunity

Starting a successful business requires preparation, special talents, skills, competencies and abilities, leadership skills as well as resources. These are critical requirements before you step into any business. Experience and observation have shown that many businesses both great and small fail because of poor or lack of preparation. You need to know that Prior Proper Preparation Prevents Poor Performance (6Ps).

So, I would like to say congratulations! The decision to start your own business can be one of the best you will ever make in your life towards economic maturity. Owning a business can be an exhilarating, inspiring, grand adventure; one full of new sights and experiences, delicious highs and occasional lows, tricky paths and, hopefully, big open skies. But to ensure that your business journey will be a fruitful one, it is important to understand the demands of what it takes to become an entrepreneur.

Setting up new business sometimes collide with the wishes of established competitors, who to get all the customers' income. Many people start their business adventure dreaming of riches and freedom and while both are certainly possible, the first thing to understand is that there are tradeoffs when you decide to start a business.

Difficult bosses, annoying coworkers, peculiar policies, demands upon your time, and limits on how much money you can make are traded for independence, creativity, opportunity, and power. But by the same token, you also swap a regular paycheck and benefits for no paycheck and no benefits. A life of security, comfort, and regularity is traded for one of uncertainty.

Start – Up Influences

Why does anybody want to take the risk of starting up their own business? It is hard work without guaranteed results. But millions do so every year around the world. The start-up is the bedrock of modern – day commercial wealth, the foundation of free-market economics upon which competition is based.

Can economists shade light on the process? Economists would tell us that new entrants into an industry can be expected when there is a rise in expected post-entry profitability for them. In other words, new entrants expect to make extra profits. Economists tell us that the rate of entry is related to the growth of the industry.

They also tell us that the entry is deterred by barriers such as high capital requirements, the existence of economies of scale, product differentiation and restricted access to necessary inputs and so on. The rate of entry is lower in industries with high degrees of concentration where it may be assumed that firms combine to deter entry. However, research also tells us that whereas the rate of small firm start-up in these concentrated industries is lower, the rate of start-up for large firms is higher.

These ideas seem to be useful, but perhaps obvious statements about start-ups, really happen. Somehow economists fail to explain convincingly the rationale for, and the process of, start-up. They seem to assume that there is a continuous flow of entrants into an industry just waiting for the possibility of extra profits. But people are not like that. They need to earn money to live and support their families.

Benefits of Owning Your Own Business or Company

Surveys show that owners of businesses or companies believe they work harder, earn more money and are happier than if they worked for someone or for a corporation. Before launching any business venture every potential entrepreneur need to consider the benefits and opportunities of business ownership.

- ## Opportunity to Gain Control Over Your Own Destiny

One of the benefits of owning their own businesses is that Entrepreneurs cite controlling their own destinies. Owning a business provides Entrepreneurs the independence and opportunity to achieve what is important to them. Entrepreneurs want to "call the shots" in their lives and they use their businesses to bring this desire to life. They reap the intrinsic rewards of knowing they are the driving forces behind their businesses.

- ## Opportunity to Reach Full Potential

Too many employees find their work boring, unchallenging and unexciting. However, to most entrepreneurs, there is little difference between work and play; and the two are synonymous. Roger Levin, founder of Levin Group, the largest dental practice management consulting firm in the world, says, "when I come to work everyday, it is not a job for me. I am having fun!" Entrepreneurs' businesses become the instrument for self – expression and self-actualization. Owning a business challenges an entrepreneur's skills, abilities, creativity and determination. The only barriers to success are self-imposed.

- ## Opportunity to Make a Difference

Increasingly, Entrepreneurs are starting businesses because they see an opportunity to make a difference in a cause that is important to them.

- ## Opportunity to Reap Unlimited Profits

Although money is not the primary force driving most Entrepreneurs, the profits their businesses can earn are an important motivating factor in their decisions to launch business ventures. If accumulating wealth is high on your list of priorities, owning a business is usually the best way to achieve it. ***Research has shown that self-employed people are four times more likely to become millionaires than those who work for someone else.***

- **Opportunity to Contribute to Society and be Recognized for Your Efforts**

Often business owners are among the most respected and most trusted of their communities. Business deals based on trust and mutual respect are the hall mark of many established businesses owned by Entrepreneurs. These Entrepreneurs enjoy the trust and the recognition they receive from the customers whom they serve faithfully over the passing of time.

- **Opportunity to Do What You Enjoy Doing**

A common sentiment among Entrepreneurs is that their business ventures don't really give them a burden instead the experience gives them excitement since most successful Entrepreneurs choose to enter particular business fields because they have an interest in them and enjoy those lines of work.

Finding Sponsorship

A safer bet as an entry wedge may be to take advantage of the willingness of someone to help sponsor the startup in some manner. Typically, the sponsor is a customer, a supplier or an investor in the startup venture. A prime requisite for all these types of sponsorship is that the sponsor is credible and likely to succeed in regard to the Entrepreneur and the venture. The strongest basis for this is usually a track record of prior accomplishment and a demonstration that the Entrepreneur possesses the capacity to perform the critical tasks of the business venture.

Acquiring a Going Concern

The final main entry strategy is to acquire a going concern. This can simplify the process of getting into business. A business can be viewed as basically a bundle of habits - customers buying, suppliers supplying, employees doing their jobs. In a going concern, those habits are already present. Expertise in a going concern should already be present in employees of the business.

Even if it is not, in a going concern the buying Entrepreneur should be able to obtain education and operating knowledge and skills from the selling owner to fill in the expertise needed. Consequently, it is fairly common to find businesses owned by Entrepreneurs who bought them with no prior experience in that particular line of business and nevertheless succeeded.

Developing a New Product or Service Opportunity

What it takes to start a company around a new product or service includes, most importantly, the discovery of an intersection between the market for that product or service and away to create one.

Creating Parallel Competition by Developing a New Product or Service

Parallel competition is often fierce. By definition it involves firms that lack strong differentiation and therefore tend to compete on price, which drives margins down. The toughness of such competition will likely force the Entrepreneur to be good at performing the functions of the business.

Franchising Opportunities

One of the best ways to start a new business, if you do it right, is to buy a franchise or other established businesses. While people typically think of Mc- Donald's, KFC, Dunkin' Donuts, or Baskin Robbins when they think of franchises, the fact is that franchises come in almost every industry. The same is true for an already established business. They can be found for sale in every industry and take a lot of the risk out of the entrepreneurship equation.

Franchising is a method of distributing services or products. With a franchise system, the franchisor (the company selling the franchise) offers its trademark and business system to the buyer, or franchisee who pays a fee for the right to do business under the franchisor's name using the franchisor's methods. The franchisee is given instructions on how to run the business as the franchisor does using the franchisor's name and the franchisor supports the franchisee with expertise, training, advertising, and a proven system.

Buying into a proven system is important. The franchises that work best are those where the franchisor has worked out the kinks and translated its business into a systematic procedure that the franchisee follows. Do what the franchisor did, and you should get the results that it got; that is the idea. As franchisors like to say, 'when you buy a franchise, you are in business for yourself but not by yourself.'

The reason that a franchise can be a smart business decision is that in the right franchise system, the franchisor has already made the mistakes so you don't have to repeat them. Franchising should reduce your risk. You need not to reinvent the wheel. In exchange for its expertise, training, and help, however, you will be required to give up some independence and do things the franchisor's way.

Finding the Right Franchise

With so many franchise systems from which to choose, the options can be dizzying. It is best to start with a global perspective. *In the universe of franchising, which industries seem to match your interests? Narrow the choices down to a few industries in which you are most interested, and then analyze your geographic area to see if there is a market for that type of business.*

Once you have decided which industry interests you most and seems to have growth potential in your area, contact all the franchise companies in that field and ask them for information. Any reputable company will be happy to send you information at no cost. A great place to learn about all of your options is at a franchise trade show. This is a terrific way to gather a lot of preliminary information and survey the field in a short period of time, and you can find them in most cities.

When attending a franchise trade show, keep a few thoughts in mind. First, remember the companies exhibiting at the show by no means make up all of the franchise opportunities available. Indeed, these events showcase only a small selection of the available franchise programs.

Analyzing the Franchisor

As you go about this research, understand that successful franchisors have certain traits in common. If you can find a franchisor that has the following traits, you are headed in the right direction;

1. The Franchisor Supports the Franchisees

The best franchises are the ones where the franchisor looks at the relationship with the franchisees as a partnership. As Steve Reinemund, the former head of Pizza Hut, puts it, ***"Franchisees are only as successful as the parent company and the parent company is only as successful as the franchisees."*** Not only do such exceptional franchisors offer plenty of communication, opportunities for growth within the company, and help during hard times, they also offer lots of advice and training.

A good example of this is Dunkin' Donuts. To support new franchisees, it created Dunkin' Donuts University. There, franchisees and their personnel are invited to attend a six-week success program that teaches them everything from basic instructions on how to run the business to how to produce the products, deal with employees, and use equipment. It even offers advice on inventory control and accounting.

The Franchisor Is Committed To Customer Service

The great franchisors do not just give lip service in customer service, they teach it to everyone in the organization, and live it on a daily basis. That is critical, because if people are treated well at other outlets, that, in turn, gives your individual franchise a good name too. As the Pizza Hut chairman put it, "We are committed to more than just good service, we are committed to providing legendary service."

The Franchisor Changes with the Times

Tastes and values change. The last thing you want is to buy into a system that is stuck in the past, not realizing that its product or service needs to adapt to the times. The better franchise systems are constantly test marketing new ideas and new products in an effort to stay ahead of the competition.

Good Franchisor's Jump Up Start Kit

This kit includes the following services;

1. Local, regional, and national advertising
2. Offer of related programs and materials
3. Field support
4. Updates to the operating manual
5. Ongoing related training for you and your management team.
6. Advisory Council
7. Research and development of new products and services
8. System enhancements
9. Communication support—an intranet, a members-only Web site
10. Monthly newsletters
11. Some other method to keep you up to date.

If the franchisor you are considering does not offer these sorts of things, it would be better for you to think twice on your option.

Location, Location, Location

Not all franchises need to pick a dynamite location. For example, janitorial services, direct mail companies, or lawn care services really donot need to worry about their location because drop-in business is not their business model. But a restaurant needs a good location. Typically, if you are looking at a retail establishment, location usually is a priority.

First, speak with the potential franchisor. One of the best aspects of buying into a good franchise operation is that you should get plenty of advice and help from the franchisor. Start there and see what it says. The franchisor will know what you should look for, what works best, and what locations are available, and the franchisor will be helping you in the site selection process. Additionally, you need to find out about territorial exclusivity.

Does the franchisor offer this and, if so, what is the size of the territory? Territorial exclusivity has been the subject of many lawsuits between franchiseesand franchisors, so make sure that you really understand this issue and have any agreements put in writing. *As always, one of the best ways to know what to expect from a franchisor on this or any subject is to talk to the current franchisees. They will tell you if the franchisor plays fair, if territorial limits are respected, and if site location analysis is accurate.*

Area Development

A topic related to location is area development. Area development allows you to open more than one franchise in a certain locale. If, for example, you want to open and buy the rights to your area en masse. This allows you to monopolize the market and excludes challengers under the same franchise umbrella from competing with you. The key things to consider regarding area development are:-Picking a franchise system that is not yet developed in the area and getting the franchisor to grant you market exclusivity.

Avoid Common Mistakes

Once all of your questions have been satisfactorily answered, you have done your due diligence and have spoken with existing franchisees, and you understand where your store will be located, it is time to sign on the dotted line. But before you do, make sure you avoid potential pitfalls. Franchisees often buy into a franchise without a full understanding of just what it takes to succeed in their chosen business. That is one of several common mistakes that are easily avoidable.

Buying an Existing Business

For many Entrepreneurs, the quickest way to enter a market is to purchase an existing business. Yet, the attraction of fast entry can be a great mistake. Buying an existing business requires a great deal of analysis and evaluation to ensure that what you are purchasing suits your needs. You do not need to rush. ***For starters, be sure that you have considered answers to the following questions:***

- Is this the type of business you would like to operate?
- Do you know the negative aspects of this type of business?
- Is this the best market for this business?
- Do you know the critical factors for this business to be successful?
- Do you have experience required to run this type of business?
- Will you need to make any changes to the business?
- If the business is currently in a decline do you have what it takes to make it profitable?
- If the business is profitable why does the current owner want to sell it?
- Have you examined other businesses that are currently for sale?

Many of these questions ask you to be honest with yourself about your ability to operate the business successfully.

Advantages of an Existing Business

1. An established successful business may continue to be successful
2. The new owner can use the experience of the previous owner
3. The new owner hits the ground running
4. An existing business may already have the best location
5. Employees and suppliers are already in place; equipment is installed and productive capacity is known and finding financing is easier.

Disadvantages an Existing Business

1. A business may be for sale because it has never been profitable
2. The previous owner may have created ill will
3. Current employees may not be suitable
4. The business location may become unnecessary
5. Equipment and facilities may be obsolete
6. Change and innovation may be difficult to implement
7. Accounts receivable may be less than the face value and sometimes the business may be overpriced.

The Potential Drawbacks of Entrepreneurship

Although owning a business has many benefits and provide many opportunities, anyone planning to enter the world of entrepreneurship should be aware of potential drawbacks.

- **Uncertainty of Income**
  Opening and running a business provides no guarantees that an entrepreneur will earn enough money to survive. Some businesses barely earn enough to provide the owner manager with an adequate income. In the early days of the business entrepreneurs often have trouble meeting financial obligations and may have to live on savings. The regularity of income that comes with working for someone is absent.

- **Risk of Losing Your Entire Invested Capital**
  The startup business failure rate is often very high. Many studies have shown that 34 percent of new businesses fail within two years and 50 percent shut down within four years. Within six years, 60 percent of new businesses will have folded.

- **Long Hours and Hard Work**
  Business startups often demand that owners keep nightmarish schedules. In many startups, 10 to 12 hour days and 6 or 7 day work – weeks with no paid vacations are the norm. Because they often must do everything themselves, owners experience intense, draining workdays.

- **Lower Quality of Life Until Business Gets Established**
  The long hours and hard work needed to launch a company can take their toll on the remainder of an Entrepreneur's life. *Business owners often find that their roles as husband and wives or fathers and mothers take a back seat to their roles as company founders for some time.*

- **High Levels of Stress**
  Launching and running a business can be a rewarding experience, but it also can be highly stressful. Most Entrepreneurs who have made significant investments in their companies, have left behind the safety and security of a steady pay check and mortgaged everything they owned to get into business. Failure means total financial ruin as well as a serious psychological blow which creates high levels of stress and anxiety.

- **Discouragement**
  Launching a business requires much dedication, discipline and tenacity. Along the way to building a successful business, Entrepreneurs will run into many obstacles, some of which may appear to be insurmountable. Discouragement and disillusionment can set in but successful Entrepreneurs know that every business

encountera rough spot and that perseverance is required to get through it.

The Ten Deadly Mistakes of Entrepreneurship

Because of limited resources, inexperienced management and lack of financial stability, many business ventures suffer a mortality rate significantly higher than that of larger established businesses. Exploring the causes of business failure may help you avoid them.

- **Lack of Experience**
  An Entrepreneur needs to have experience in the field he or she wants to enter. For example, if a person wants to open a retail clothing business, he should first work in a retail clothing store. This will give him or her practical experience as well as help him or her learn the nature of business. This type of experience can spell the difference between failure and success.

  Ideally, *a prospective Entrepreneur should have adequate technical ability; a working knowledge of the physical operations of the business; sufficient conceptual ability; the power to visualize, coordinate and integrate the various operations of the business into a synergistic whole and skill to manage people in the organization and motivate them to higher levels of performance.*

- **Management Incompetence**
  In most business ventures management inexperience or poor decision-making ability is the chief problem of the failing enterprise. The owner lacks leadership ability and knowledge necessary to make the business work.

- **Undercapitalization**
  Sound management is the key to entrepreneurial success and effective managers realize that any successful business venture requires proper financial control. The margin for error in managing

finances is especially small for most Entrepreneurs and neglecting to install proper financial controls is a recipe for disaster. *Two pitfalls affecting entrepreneurs' business financial health are common: undercapitalization and poor cash management.*

Many Entrepreneurs make the mistake of beginning their businesses on a "shoestring" which is a fatal error leading to business failure. Entrepreneurs tend to be overly optimistic and often underestimate the financial requirements of launching a business or the amount of time required for the business or company to become self – sustaining. As a result, they start off undercapitalized and can never seem to catch up financially as their companies consume increasing amounts of cash to fuel growth.

- **Poor Cash Management**
  Insufficient Cash Flow due to poor cash management is a common cause of business failure. Companies need adequate cash flow to thrive, without it, a company will go out of business. Maintaining adequate cash flow and to pay bills in a timely fashion is a constant challenge for most entrepreneurs especially those in a startup phase or more established companies experiencing growth.

  Fast – growing companies devour cash fast! Poor credit and collection practices on accounts receivables, sloppy accounts payable practices that exert undue pressure on a company's cash balance and uncontrolled spending are common to many business ventures bankruptcies.

- **Lack of Strategic Management**
  Too many Entrepreneurs neglect the process of strategic management because they think that it is something that only benefits large companies. "I do not have the time" or "We are too small to develop a strategic plan," they often rationalize. *Failure to plan usually results in failure to survive.* Without a clear defined strategy, a business has no sustainable basis for creating and maintaining a competitive edge in the market place.

- **Weak Market Effort**

  Business success requires a sustained, creative marketing effort to draw a base of customers and to keep them coming back. Creative Entrepreneurs find ways to market their businesses effectively to their target customers without breaking the bank.

- **Uncontrolled Growth**

  Growth is a natural, healthy and desirable part of any business enterprise but it must be planned and controlled. Peter Drucker says that startup companies can expect to outgrow their capital bases each time sales increase 40 to 50 percent. Ideally Entrepreneurs finance the expansion of their companies by the profits they generate ("retained earnings") or by capital contributions from the owners, but most businesses end up borrowing at least a portion of the capital investment.

- **Poor Location**

  For any business, choosing the right location is partly an art and partly a science. Too often entrepreneurs select their locations without adequate research and investigation. Some beginning owners choose a particular location just because they noticed a vacant building. But the location principle is too critical to leave to chance. There is also need to consider the rate of rent. A location has two important features: what it costs and what it generates in the sales volume.

- **Inability to Make the "Entrepreneurial Transition"**

  If a business fails, it is most likely to do so in its first five years of life. Making it over the "entrepreneurial startup hump," however, is no guarantee of business success. After the startup, growth usually requires a radically different style of leadership and management.

  Many businesses fail when their founders are unable to make the transition from Entrepreneur to manager and are unwilling to bring professional management. The very abilities that make an Entrepreneur successful often lead to managerial ineffectiveness. Growth requires Entrepreneurs to delegate authority and to relinquish hands – on control to daily operations, something many Entrepreneurs simply cannot do. Their business's success requires that they avoid micromanaging and become preservers and promoters of their companies' vision, mission, core values and culture.

Putting Failure into Perspective

Because Entrepreneurs are building businesses in an environment filled with uncertainty and shaped by rapid change.They recognize that failure is likely to be part of their lives and they do not get paralyzed by that recognition. "The excitement of building a new business from scratch is far greater than the fear of failure." Says, one Entrepreneur who failed several times before finally succeeding.

Successful Entrepreneurs have the attitude that failures are simply stepping stones along the path of success. This leads to a conclusion that failure is a natural part of the creative process. The only people who never fail are those who never do anything or never attempt anything new. One hall mark of successful Entrepreneurs is the ability to fail intelligently, learning why they failed so that they can avoid making the same mistake again.

They know that business success does not depend on their ability to avoid making mistakes but to be open to the lessons each mistake brings. They learn from their failures and use them as fuel to push themselves closer to their ultimate target. Entrepreneurs are less worried about what they might lose if they try something and fail than about what they miss if they fail to try. The entrepreneurial success requires both persistence and resilience, the ability to bounce back from failures.

How to Avoid the Pitfalls

As valuable as failure can be to the entrepreneurial process, no one sets out to fail. We have seen some of the most common reasons behind business failures. Now we must examine the ways to avoid becoming another failure statistic and gain insight into what makes a startup successful. Entrepreneurial success requires much more than just a good idea for a product or service.

It also takes solid plan execution, adequate resources such as capital and people, the ability to assemble and manage those resources and perseverance. Strategies to avoid the pitfalls include: knowing your business in depth; preparing a good business plan; managing financial resources well; understanding financial statements; managing people effectively; having a competitive advantage over rivals; leveraging (doing more with the less) and financial intelligence.

CHAPTER 3

Start With What You Have

This is a chapter that encourages anyone who has a burning desire to start a business but he or she has insufficient startup capital. My advice to you is, do not worry, start with what you have. Three things are important at this level. First, you must have a clear strategic vision answering three strategic questions: where am I? Where do I want to be? and how do I get there? Second, is to craft a mission statement clearly explaining the business scope which must answer the following questions: who we are? what we do? and why are we in business? Third is the financial education from which you will be able to use financial intelligence.

On one hand while strategic vision is the description of the road map or the unfolding of your tomorrow, it is simply an idea. On the other hand, it is the financial intelligence that solves money problems which includes the lack of adequate capital to start your own business.

You can emulate my example.

When I decided to be a writer, I just started writing. Then I finally realized the obvious: if you want to be a writer, start writing! Writing is free, and no one needs to bestow a title of writer upon you to begin writing. The same is true with art, business, travel, and plenty of other fields.

If you want to start a business, all you need is one idea. The idea doesnot need to be big; sometimes small ideas make great small businesses. Think about one thing you know how to do that other people would also like to know about. This means that, *to identify what type of business you will be able to do, is simple and easy. Just do research and find out the problem that is in your area and think about the solution to that problem. It is that solution that will turn to be your greatest idea from which you can base your decision to start your own business.*

Use What You Have

One day I was reading a book and the writer said,"My biggest challenge is in keeping focused on myself and avoiding the unhelpful comparison with others. I know it is essential to do this and yet it is incredibly hard to practice". Based on what this writer said I can conclude that the death of contentment is comparison.

Comparisons are generally unhelpful since:

1) We are only likely to compare ourselves to others whose achievements dwarf our own and hence make ourselves feel bad in the process. It would be fine if we sought their example as inspiration to work hard to get there, but most people (myself included) use the comparison as a means of beating ourselves up for not being where we would like to be.

2) We only see the publically shared information that represents the highs, the good-points and the accomplishments. Nobody really shares the downs, the failures or the difficulties, only the bits they are proud of which will inflate their ego. If only we could remember this when comparing ourselves to them, we might feel better about how we measure up.

3) We donot recognize all the years of hard work, disappointments, the failures and the occasional good-fortune that resulted in their achievements.

Using what we have means maintaining an inward focus on making the best use of our own time, skills, potential and attention rather than being driven by factors outside of our influence. Progress towards our goals each day, depends on how we apply our skills, time and resources, the actions we take, the decisions we make and the distractions we resist. It all comes down to us.

Do What You Can

Resisting distraction and comparison, focusing attention upon taking action and accepting our starting point as the launching pad for the process of creation are all essential if we are to free ourselves to take action and get on with the process of doing business.

Sure, we may wish for more favorable conditions. Our starting point may be non-ideal. Progress so far may well have been rocky, or non-existent to this point. Regardless of all these factors, we have the choice to accept them and to act regardless, or to use them as further sources of despondency and justifications for inaction.It is a battle I fight with myself daily, but I know that it feels better when I choose the path of action. I hope the same is true to you. A common question many of us ask is this: How do I get from where I am to where I want to be if there is nothing to build on in the first place?

For example, you want to start a business, but you have no experience in business development. You want to shift to a different career field, but you donot have knowledge in the area. You want to be at the top in what you do but you have no know-how in the area. You want to let go of your past and start on a new journey, but there is nothing for you to start off with. And if you cannot create something, you cannot get anything.

If you have ever felt this way about your goals, there are a few points I want to share with you.

There Are Many Successful People Who Start From Nothing

The first thing I want to point out is that many people start from nothing. While there are rich people who start from a position of power and wealth, there are many successful people from poor families, just as there are people who lead lackadaisical lives despite having a lot of wealth. Instead of talking about money here, I want to focus the discussion on one's personal achievements and knowledge, because these are arguably what shapes one's life success.

The second point I want to make is to invite you to rethink the notion that you have nothing. Because every time you think you have nothing, it is likely the opposite. It is the proverbial notion of whether the glass is half-empty or half-full. There is always something there. The pessimist sees the glass as half-empty; the optimist sees the glass as half-full.

Have you ever considered that the glass has always been all full though? The bottom half is filled with water, and the top half is filled with air. If you donot see what you have today as something, it is possible that you have been living in your own reality for too long, to the point where you take what you have for granted. You have developed a mental blindness to the value of what you have. It is a matter of re-tuning yourself to recognize those things you do have.

Try mentally swapping positions with someone who is in a worse-off situation than you. It can be someone who just got robbed, someone who just got retrenched, a convict sentenced for life behind bars, a patient suffering from a terminal illness with a month to live, a vegetable, a person with anterograde amnesia, a starving beggar with no home to go to, a bankrupt, someone with heavy debt to clear, a famine-stricken child in Africa, etc. — the possibilities are endless. How would you feel? What would you become? What would life be like compared to what you have now?

Suddenly, it is apparent that there are so many things in your life you didnot realize. All the things you have from before that you saw as nothing suddenly becomes something. Things like your senses, your health, your freedom, your livelihood, your rights, your friends, your family, your knowledge, your skill sets, your abilities, your intellect, and many more elements begin to make sense.

All these are real things, real tools that you possess. They are assets beyond any doubt. There are many people who wish they had these, yet they donot. Realize it or not, by being able to see this post, you are in a better place than many people in this world. ***And focusing on the things that you do have now and making the best out of them are surer ways to move you forward in life than not recognizing them.***

Your Problems Are Something Too

In fact, everything you have in your life now is something. Including your problems, contrary to what many would think. I know many of you may be thinking, '*how can my problems be of value? They weigh me down. I wish I could get rid of all my life problems immediately.*'

There was something I read in ***Think and Grow Rich*** years ago that I want to share with you. Many people always see their problems as liabilities, and the things they have as assets. However, have you ever realized that your problems are actually your assets too — in fact, bigger assets than you realize? Because for every problem you face, hundreds of thousands of people around the world are probably facing it too. And if your problem is so huge that it's weighing on you, imagine how many people would want to know the solution to this problem. Who is a better person to discover the solution than you, the person who is in the middle of it all?

Once you find the solution, imagine how valuable this solution will be to others who have the same problem. It is a huge asset! ***Your problems are really your assets in disguise. They are your hidden gold mines waiting to be mined and converted into gold.*** In fact, our problems are the keys to abundance. It is with these problems that you become a richer person, not just in terms of physical wealth, but also emotionally, mentally and spiritually.

And Then There Is Something Else

And even beyond your problems/liabilities, assets, knowledge, abilities, and skill sets, there is something else that you have. Even if you have nothing to your name, even if you have been declared bankrupt, even if you are million dollars in debt, even if everyone has left you in this world, even if you are to lose your job/status/knowledge/achievements, even if your life has been decimated, you still have something.

Chapter 4

Develop a Great Product or Service

The quality of your product or service determines 90% of business success. Quality is the key determining factor of your growth and profitability. It is mothers your reputation. How often customers say: "This is a great product or service!"

To this end you need to decide what exactly you intend to sell. Some questions include: what does your customer consider valuable and is willing to pay for it? What will be the best compliments that you receive from your happy customer? What will your products offer to your customers that make them superior to your competitors? What will your products or services offer to your customers that will make them superior to your competitors? What products or services should you abandon or discontinue because you cannot achieve excellence in those areas? The market only rewards excellent products and services.

Although production is a necessary economic activity, some people overrate its importance in relation to marketing. Production and marketing are both important parts of a total business system aimed at providing consumers with need-satisfying goods and services. Simply put, take out marketing there will be no production. Together, production and marketing supply five kinds of economic utility:

- Form Utility

Form Utility is provided when someone produces something tangible (things you can touch or see).

- Task Utility

Task Utility is provided when someone performs a task for someone else. Thus, marketing decisions focus on the customer and include decisions about what goods and services to produce. It doesnot make sense to provide goods and services consumers donot want when they are so many things that they want.

Marketing is concerned with what customers want – and should guide what is produced and offered. Even when marketing and production are combined to provide form or task utility, consumers can not be satisfied until possession, time and place utility are also provided.

- Possession Utility

Possession Utility means obtaining goods or services and having the right to use or consume them.

- Time Utility

Time Utility means having the product available WHEN the customer wants.

- Place Utility

This Means having the product available WHERE the customer wants.

CHAPTER 5

Understanding Markets

Marketing is both a philosophy of business and an important function in the operation of a company. Marketing is concerned with making profits by providing customers satisfaction. ***Thus, when people buy products or services they do not want the products or service per se, they want the benefits from using the products or services.***Products and services help to solve customers' problems. It is the solutions to these problems that customers are really buying.

Development of Present-Day Marketing

In early industrial and commercial developments, the emphasis was placed on production. Demand was high and all that was manufactured could be sold without difficulty. Later the emphasis switched to sales. With reduction in consumer demand, effort had to be made to sell factory output

Roughly the period from the 1920s to the 1950s, was characterized by this sales orientation. Thus, sales and advertising were the activities receiving most emphasis. Latter from the 1950s to the present day with ever increasing competitor activity and consumer needs and wants should initiate the production process.

Thus, a marketing orientation developed and this is the current situation. However, it is important to recognize that not all organizations adapted the marketing orientation and, in most cases, corporate failure can be directly attributed to companies having a production orientation approach.

Characteristics of Organizations Having Production Orientation

- ✓ Demand is a function of supply
- ✓ There is an emphasis on production
- ✓ The firm has an inward-looking approach
- ✓ Most things made can be sold
- ✓ Buyers are sensitive to price
- ✓ Market must have low cost
- ➢ With sales orientation, selling the output of production becomes the most important activity

Characteristics of Organization Having Marketing Orientation

- • Scarcity of markets
- • A focus on customers
- • An outward looking approach
- • High level of competitor activity
- • Supply exceeds demand

Organizations adopting a marketing orientation or the marketing concept are therefore interested in the satisfaction of consumer needs and wants at a profit.

The Market Concept

Marketing concept is concerned with satisfying consumer needs and wants at a profit. Therefore, business is about satisfying customers at a profit. So, any company implementing the marketing concept will achieve their corporate objectives by identifying and satisfying the needs and want of a target markets more effectively than competitors. Effective marketing starts with the recognition of customer needs and then works backwards to devise products or services to satisfy these needs.

In this way marketing managers can satisfy customers more efficiently in the present and anticipate changes in customer needs more accurately in the future. This means that organizations should focus on building long term customer relations in which the initial sale is viewed as a beginning step in the process, not as an end goal.

What Marketing is all about?

Marketing is defined as the process of planning and executing conception, pricing, promotion and distribution of ideas, goods and services to create exchanges that satisfy individual and organizational goals.

Marketing is the performance of activities that seek to accomplish an organization's objectives by anticipating customer or client needs and directing a flow of need satisfying goods and services from producer to customer or client. Marketing is the management process responsible for identifying, anticipating and satisfying consumers' requirements profitably. Therefore, marketing is more than selling and advertising.

The Marketing Mix

Marketing involves making a number of interrelated decisions about various aspects of company activity, which have a major impact on success or failure of the company as a business enterprise. The term marketing mix is used to denote the range of activities within the framework of marketing decision making.

The marketing mix is the set of controllable variables that must be managed to satisfy the target market and achieve organizational objectives. For convenience, the market mix is divided into four major decision areas: Product Decisions, Price Decisions, Promotion Decisions and Place Decisions

Product Decisions

- These include the number, type, brand grouping and quality of company products, their sizes, variety and form of packing.
- Decisions on whether to add new products, phase out products, restyle or rebrand fall into this category.

2. Price Decisions

- These include the discount structure, the relationship of price between product sizes, the general pricing policy and the pricing of new products.

3. Promotion Decisions

- These include advertising strategy, media selection, copy writing, public relations, personal selling and special sales promotions, all involving the conveyance of information about the company

4. Place Decisions

- These include decisions relating to the distribution channels and the appointment of agents among other things

The effective use of the marketing tools within the marketing mix is an interrelated manner and is the key to successful marketing and profitable business.

Marketing Management

We have identified the main elements of the marketing mix as: Product; Price; Promotion and Place. The aim of marketing management is to get the right product of the right quality to right place at the right price using the right promotional methods. Marketing management is therefore the process of putting into practice the marketing mix-known as the 4Ps.

To manage this process it involves analysis, planning and control:

1. Analysis

As we have seen, a marketing orientation begins and ends with the customer. Thus, analysis in marketing management involves finding the answers to the following questions:

- ✓ Who are our customers and potential customers?
- ✓ Who do they buy (or not buy)
- ✓ Do they buy our product or service?
- ✓ When do they buy it?
- ✓ Where do they buy it?
- ✓ How do they buy it?
- ✓ Having bought the product are they satisfied with it?
- ✓ How are customer needs changing?
- ✓ Which of the competitor's products do they consider buying?

2. Planning

Marketing management also involves using the information gained from market analysis to plan the organization's marketing response/activities.

3. Control

The third main component of marketing management is to control the operationalization of the marketing plan. Control involves setting measurable targets for the plan and then checking performance against these targets. If necessary, remedial action will need to be taken to ensure that planned and actual performances are brought into line.

Internal Marketing

As part of the overall marketing process of delivering customer satisfaction it is important that the whole corporate effort is coordinated and committed to achieving this objective. In practice, this means that all employees at all levels should appreciate not only the reason for the firm's existence; but also that each and every employee has a responsibility to understand the concept of customer or marketing orientation and the importance of their individual contribution.

CHAPTER 6

Attract and Retain High Performing People in your Business

A Link between Entrepreneurship and Human Resource Management

This chapter conveys concepts and principles of Human Resource Management (HRM) in connection with Entrepreneurship. Many HRM scholars point out that HRM covers: the definition of HRM; the matching model of HRM; the HRM policies; the aims and objectives of HRM and HRM theory; the characteristics of HRM; the development of HRM as an approach to managing people, even in a business environment; approaches to HRM –Soft Vs Hard; current and future challenges to HRM and the context within which HRM functions, and the ethical dimensions that effect HR policy and practice. We will therefore look at a few of them.

Human Resource Management Defined

Many business commentators say that Human Resource Management is a productive use of people to achieve strategic business objectives and satisfy individual employee needs. According to Armstrong (2009) Human Resource Management is a strategic, integrated and coherent approach to the employment, development and wellbeing of the people working in organizations.

However, other scholars say that human resource management involves all management decisions and action that affect the nature of the relationship between the organization and its employees – its human resources. Boxall et al (2007) describe HRM as the management of work and people towards desired ends. Boxall et al (2007) believe that HRM can be regarded as a set of interrelated policies with an ideological and philosophical underpinning. This means that HRM comprises a set of policies designed to maximize organizational integration, employee commitment, flexibility and quality of work.

Therefore, it can be concluded that HRM consists of the following propositions:

- That human resource policies should be integrated with strategic business planning
- That human resource management is a distinct approach to employment management which seeks to achieve competitive advantage through the strategic deployment of a highly committed and capable workforce
- That HRM is concerned with how a company or organizations manage their workforce

People Resourcing Strategy

People Resourcing Strategy (PRS) is concerned with taking steps to ensure that the organization attracts and retains the people it needs and employ them efficiently. PRS is closely associated with learning and developed strategy, which sets out how the organization ensures that it has the skilled and knowledgeable workforce it needs.

The Objectives of PRS

The concept that the strategic capability of a firm depends on its resource capability in the shape of people (resource-based view) provides the rationale for resourcing strategy. This strategy is to ensure that a firm achieves competitive advantage by attracting and retaining more capable people than its rivals and employing them more effectively.

The Strategic HRM approach to Resourcing

Strategic HRM emphasizes the importance of human resources in achieving organizational capability and therefore the need to find people whose attitudes and behavior are likely to be congruent with what management believes to be appropriate and conducive to success.

Additionally, strategic HRM emphasizes using a systematic approach, starting with human resource planning and proceeding through recruitment and selection, followed by performance management, learning and development, recognition and reward.

Integrating Business and Resource Strategies

The philosophy behind the strategic HRM approach to resourcing is that it is people who implement the strategic plan.

Considerations affecting the integration of business and resourcing strategies;

- The numbers of people required to support the achievement of business strategies.
- The skills and behavior required to support the achievement of business strategies.

The Components of People Resource Strategy

- **Human Resource Planning** - workforce planning
- **Retention Strategy** - preparing plans for retaining the people the organization needs
- **Absence management strategy** - planning for the control of absence
- **Flexibility Strategy** - planning for increased productivity in the use of human resources to enable the organization to make the best use of people)

- **Talent Management Strategy** – ensuring that the organization has the talented people it requires to provide for management succession and meet present and future business needs
- **Engagement Strategy** – planning the approaches used to attract people

Human Resource Planning (HRP)

The focus of Human Resource Planning (HRP) or employment planning is on the demand and supply of labour. *HRP involves the acquisition, development and departure of people (employees) and it is the responsibility of all managers and not just the HR department.*

The success of an organization depends on its employees. This means that its competitiveness and ultimate survival depends on having the right people in the right jobs at the right times.

HRP therefore is concerned with the flow of people into, through and out of the organization. It is the process of ensuring that the human resource requirements of an organization are identified and plans are made for satisfying those requirements

Armstrong (2009) points out that HRP involves facilitating the acquisition, utilization, development and retention of company's human resources. According to Armstrong (2009) a distinction can be made between 'hard' and soft HRP. The former is based on quantitative analysis to ensure that the right number of the right sort of people is available when needed.

Aims of HRP

Armstrong (2009) says HRP aims to ensure that the organization has the number of people with the right skills needed to meet forecast requirements. This means that HRP is important because it encourages employers to develop clear and explicit links between their business and HR plans and to integrate the two more effectively.

It allows for better control over staffing costs and numbers employed, and it enables employers to make more informed judgments about the skills and attitude mix in organization. HRP also provides a profile of current staff in terms of age, sex, disability, so as to move towards being an equal opportunity organization.

Approaches to HRP

HRP involves the activities listed below:

a) **Scenario planning** – making broad assessments of the future environmental factors and their likely impact on people requirements.

b) **Demand forecasting** – estimating future needs for people and competences by reference to corporate and functional plans and forecasts of future activity levels.

c) **Supply forecasting** - estimating the supply of people by reference to analyses of current resources and future availability.

d) **Forecasting requirements** – analyze demand and supply forecasts to identify future deficits or surpluses with the help of models, where appropriate

e) **Action planning** – prepare plans to deal with forecast deficits through internal promotion, training or external recruitment

CHAPTER 7

Location and Facilities Layout

Locating a business in the right place is important because the cost of moving output and people across space is significant. For example, the best site for a retail store generally is one that is in close proximity to a large number of people who are the potential customers of the store.In contrast a manufacturing firm may combine raw materials from several sources and ship manufactured output to customers at other sites. In this case, an important location criterion is the cost of shipping raw material relative to the cost of shipping final output. Another consideration is that all firms employ workers who must travel from their homes to the firm each working day.

An Entrepreneur's ultimate goal is to locate the business at a site that will maximize the likelihood of success. The more Entrepreneurs invest in researching potential locations the higher is the probability that they will find the spot that is best suited for the company. The trick is to keep an open mind about where the location of the business might be.

Consideration in selecting the best location should consider the following questions: whether the business should be closer to the customer or closer to the supplier (raw material source) or in the center between the customer and supplier. Additionally, the cost of shipping the input and output should also be considered. Amongst location decisions the entrepreneur must also consider locating the firm in close proximity to that labour supply or face the prospect of paying premium wages to compensate workers for travelling long distances and/ or providing housing.

Facilities Design and Layout

A facility is defined as the workspace and equipment needed to carry out the operations of the organization. This includes offices, factories, computers, and trucks. The location, design, and layout of an organization's facilities are central to maximizing the efficiency of the overall operations system.

Facilities layout design refers to the arrangement of all equipment, machinery, and furnishing within a building envelope after considering the various objectives of the facility. The layout consists of production areas, support areas, and the personnel areas in the building. The need for facilities layout design arises both in the process of designing a new layout and in redesigning an existing layout.

The need in the former case is obvious but in the latter case it is because of many developments as well as many problems within the facility such as change in the product design, obsolescence of existing facilities, change in demand, frequent accidents, more scrap and rework, market shift, introduction of a new product, etc.

Objectives of Facilities Layout Design

Primary objectives of a typical facility layout include

(1) Overall integration and effective use of man, machine, material, and supporting services
(2) Minimization of material handling cost by suitably placing the facilities in the best possible way
(3) Better supervision and control
(4) Employees convenience, safety, improved morale and better working environment
(5) Higher flexibility and adaptability to changing conditions
(6) Waste minimization and higher productivity.

The basic types of layouts are:

• Product layout • Process layout • Fixed position layout • Cellular layout.

After choosing the facility's location, the next stage in operations planning is to design the best physical layout for the facility. The available space needs to be assessed with workstations, equipment, storage, and other amenities need to be arranged. The aim is to allow for the most efficient workflow without disruption. A workplace that has carefully arranged its layout will allow for a more effective and efficient workflow and produce its good or services to a high standard.

Facility Layout Considerations

Facility Entrepreneurs should consider several factors when designing the layout of a facility to achieve maximum effectiveness.

- Does the design and layout allow for growth or change? Is there a chance that your company will experience significant growth? Could some other changes come about that could influence the layout of your facility? In business, anything is possible. Make sure that same is true of your facilities layout. While making changes is a costly, undertaking them shouldn't be taken lightly, your layout should be flexible enough to allow a redesign if the situation calls for it.
- Is the process flow smooth? If you are running a factory, for example, the flow should be such that the raw materials enter at one end and the finished product exits at the other. The flow doesnot have to form a straight line, but there should be no backtracking. Backtracking creates confusion. Employees get confused ("Has that been done yet?"), parts get lost, and coordination is very difficult. You need to have a smooth process to be efficient.
- Are materials being handled efficiently? Here simplicity is best.
- Does the facility layout aid the business in meeting its production needs? Is there enough space and is it used efficiently? Have you allowed enough space for shipping and receiving? Can different areas of the business communicate effectively? Does the layout lend itself to promotional activities? (e.g., showing the facilities to potential customers).
- Does the layout contribute to employee satisfaction and moral? Numerous studies have linked employee moral to productivity. So, managers should take this point into consideration when designing

the layout of their facilities. How can this be done? Paint the walls light colors, allow for windows and space, and include a cafeteria and a gym. ***Some of the options may cost lots of money, but if it increases productivity in the long run, it is probably worth making the investment.***

The Principal of Median Location

The principle of median location helps to explain the concentration of businesses at particular points. This principle of median location is one reason why the urban centers in the world have grown so much in the past fifty years. These cities are the medial, or at least central,locations for many types of economic activity. For example, often stores are found at the median location at center of the market area. Obviously, one finds stores scattered at various points in urban and even rural areas.

However, the growth of urban centers suggests a strong tendency to locate businesses at or near the median location within those markets. Therefore, a firm serving a liner market should locate at the median location, where there are an equal number of customers on both sides of the firm. Such a location will minimize total transport costs associated with serving those customers

If two firms serve a liner market where buyers are evenly dispersed along the market and demand does not vary with the seller's location both will tend to locate at the midpoint. Because of additional loading and unloading costs, firms tend not to locate at points intermediate between raw material sources and markets.

In general, products that tend to be weight losing in the production processes are associated with locations at the site of the raw materials. For example, the processing of gravel involves screening and washing quantities of rock, dirt and other debris to separate that part of the load that qualities as gravel

Locational Factors in Real World Situation

Obviously, the process used by managers to select location for a plant is more involving than that suggested by the preceding theoretical discussion but the process is consistent with theory.In general, all significant factors that will influence the profitability are evaluated at each location under consideration. Because both revenue and cost may differ at each location, the analysis must consider each location's attributes as they affect these two variables.

The locational attributes described here are fundamental in the decision to locate an industrial facility. Although for particular firms, some are more important than others, a significant shortfall in an area's ability to provide even one of these may greatly reduce the attractiveness of that site.

Chapter 8

Financing the Business

Decide on Business Finance:
Equity or Debt

In financial reporting we normally deal with financial statements that an organization's accounting system produces. This includes the profit and loss account also commonly called Income Statement, the balance sheet and cash flow statements. The income statement presents the financial performance, the statement of financial position also called balance sheet presents the financial position while cash flow represents the financial adaptability. Out of the three financial statements the balance sheet which represents assets, capital and liabilities shows how the business is financed.

Show me the Money

Finding the funds to start your business is usually one of the most challenging things the budding Entrepreneur will face. Whether yours is a small, home-based business or a large venture that requires six- or seven-figure funding, the good news is that money is available. The bad news is that it is sometimes harder to secure than you may anticipate. But look around. Every one of those businesses that you see as you drive down the street began as someone's dream and, somehow, those Entrepreneurs found the money to open their doors. If they did, so can you.

New businesses normally have difficult time securing start – up capital for a variety of reasons. Conventional financing may be difficult because a new business is a risk to Banks—there is no track record or assets to go on. For this reason, almost 75 percent of all startup businesses are funded through other means. In this chapter, those other options are examined.

Money and the New Business

The very first thing required of you is to accurately estimate the amount of money you need. Taking a cold, hard look at your money requirements will help you know your business better and help ensure your success. Once you know how much capital your business will require, it will be incumbent on you to get it. Having a cash crunch from the start is a sure way to go out of business fast. Moreover, a realistic budget will help convince a lender or investor that you understand your business and are worth the risk. *The first thing any investor will want to know is how much money you will need and how you plan to spend it. They will be interested to know the specific details on how the money will be spent and how you plan to repay the money.*

How much money do you need?

If you have created a business plan, you should have a pretty good idea how much money you will need to get started. If you havenot figured it out yet, this section will help you. *The money you will need can be divided into three categories: one-time costs, working capital, and ongoing costs.* One-time costs are things that you will need to spend money on to start your business but will unlikely see again, such as: Legal and accounting costs. You may need to hire a lawyer to help you negotiate contracts, incorporate, or perform other legal services.

An accountant may be needed to set up your books.Working capital is the money you will need to keep your business going until you start to make a profit. The old adage *"it takes money to make money"* is true and real. It is critical to have enough working capital on hand to cover the following costs: Debt payments. If you will be borrowing money to get started, you will want to begin repaying it right away. Service businesses have little, if any inventory, but retail and wholesale companies often spend large sums in this area.

Business finance therefore deals with deciding the capital structure. Capital structure explains how the business is financed. Businesses are either financed by equity capital or debt capital. These are the main sources of finance. However, each of these has cost of acquisitioning the funds. Thus, if funds are acquired from equity holders the business will pay cost of equity to its shareholders and if funds have been acquired from lenders of finance such as banks the business pays cost of debt normally with an interest.

Although debt is a way of financing a business, in many cases, the financial institutions such as banks do not provide the funds to a newly established business because normally Banks look for financial statement or collateral of which the business might not have because it is just starting. So, this leaves only one option of financing the business that is just starting with equity funds.

Since there are two options for financing the business: equity or debt, you can also decide to obtain the funds from both equity holders (your own funds) and the Banks at the same time. Therefore, in most cases, a company's funds may be viewed as a pool of resource, that is, a combination of different funds with different costs. Under such circumstances, it might seem appropriate to use an average cost of capital for investment approval. Weighted average cost of capital is the average cost of company's finance (equity, debentures, Bank loans,etc,) weighted according to the proportion each element bears to the total pool of capital. Weighting is usually based on market valuations, current yields and cost after tax. However, the question is that higher level of borrowing increases the financial risk and this must be avoided.

CHAPTER 9

Understanding Legal Environment of Business

Administration of Justice

Nature of Law

The word 'law' may be used in different senses: we often speak of the 'laws' of economics, laws of science or laws of morals. *Many law experts define law as rules of conduct imposed by a state upon its members and enforced by the courts.* This means that law consists of any principle which is recognized and enforced by the courts in the administration of justice. The law of a particular state is therefore a body of rules designed to regulate human conduct within that state

Broadly speaking there are three types of rules:

(a) Rules which forbid certain types of behavior under threat of penalty
(b) Rules which require people to compensate others whom they injure in certain ways
(c) Rules which specify what must be done to order certain types of human activity. For example to form a company

Although it is inevitable that the courts will make some rules, Parliament is the sovereign body

- It can therefore impose new rules or abolish any existing rules
- The basic role of the courts is to interpret these rules, decide whether they have been broken and pass sentence or make an award of compensation

Classification of Laws

There are many ways to classify law, the most fundamental distinction being that drawn between criminal and civil law. On one hand Criminal Law is law concerned with rules of conduct imposed by the state on the individual. Its objective is to punish the wrong doer and suppress crime. Civil Law is concerned with wrongs done against an individual.

The system of courts is divided into dealing with civil matters and those dealing with criminal matters. Criminal and Civil hearings take place in different courts with different rules of procedure. There is also different standard of proof. In a criminal trial the prosecution must prove the accused guilt beyond reasonable doubt.

Business Law: Law of Contract

What Contract is all about?

A contract is an agreement between two or more parties that creates obligation on them that law will recognize and enforce. *All contracts are agreements but not all agreements are contracts.*The enforceability of the agreement arises from the moral premise that an individual who voluntarily assumes an obligation that creates expectations in others should fulfill that obligation. If he does not do so, the other party should be allowed to recover compensation for any loss or damage that he may suffer because of the non – fulfillment of the obligation so assumed. Thus, for there to be a valid contract, there must be at least the following five (5) essentials:

Essentials of a Valid Contract

Agreement

An agreement which is enforceable as a contract may be oral or in writing. This is because there are generally no legal requirements that an agreement should be in writing for it to be treated by law as a legally binding contract. As a result, an agreement will be enforced by law as a contract even though it is not in writing at all. In fact, the largest number of contracts are never in writing. They are oral. The method which the courts determine whether an agreement has been reached is to enquire whether one party has made an offer which the other party has accepted. As stated earlier for most types of contract, the offer and acceptance may be made orally in writing or they may be implied from the conduct of the parties.

Offer

An offer can be described as an expression of willingness by one person (the Offeror) to enter into a contract with another person (the Offeree) made with an intention that it should be binding on the Offeror as soon as it is accepted by the Offeree. Thus, if for example, A person goes into a shop, picks up a bottle of coke and walks to the paying counter with money in his hands. That is an offer to buy the drink. Consequently, if the shop attendant accepts the money in payment for the coke, a contract will have been concluded between him and the shop for the sale of the Coke.

Invitation to Offers

However, it should be noted that not every apparent offer will be regarded as such by law. Some words or conduct which may appear to be offers are not offers at all. For example, an advertisement of goods for sale is not an offer of the goods for sale. Similarly, the display of goods in a shop window or on a shop shelf is also not an offer of the goods for sale.

Termination of an Offer

An offer will not constitute an agreement unless it is accepted before it is terminated by the Offeror. As a result, where the Offeree purports to accept an offer that has already been terminated, his/her acceptance will not be valid to convert the offer into an agreement between him and the Offeror. An offer can be terminated through the following ways:

(a) Counter Offer
(b) Revocation
(c) Rejection
(d) Lapse of Time
(e) Un occurrence of an event

Acceptance

An offer cannot constitute an agreement unless it is first accepted by the Offeree. In other words, it is the combination of an offer and acceptance that creates an agreement which will be enforced as a contract. *Under the law of contract, an acceptance is defined as a final and unqualified expression of assent to the terms of an offer.*

Communication of Acceptance

Generally, an acceptance must be communicated to the Offeror so that in the absence of that, there will be no contract. In other words, the acceptance must be brought to the Offeror's notice. Accordingly, there is no contract where the Offeree writes his acceptance of the offer on a piece of paper which he keeps himself.

Consideration

Although there may be a valid agreement constituted by an offer which is accepted, the agreement may not be enforced as a contract in the absence of 'consideration'. Consideration shall mean something of value in the eyes of law. The basis of this rule is the fact that courts are not willing to enforce gratuitous promises as contracts.

For this purpose, consideration is either some benefit to the Offeror or some detriment to the Offeree. Thus, payment by the buyer is consideration for the seller's delivery. Conversely, delivery or promise of delivery by the seller is consideration for the buyer's payment or promise of payment. This can be described either as a detriment to the seller or as a benefit to the buyer

In law of contract past, consideration is no consideration at all. For this reason, payment for past services is generally not contractually binding as valid consideration unless the services were rendered on the premise that the payment would be made at some future date

Privity of Contract

Because of the importance of consideration in the enforcement of a contract, generally only parties to a contract will be allowed to enforce it. In other words, a person who is not a party to contract (i.e. who has not provided consideration) will not be allowed to enforce the contract even if it was concluded for his benefit. For example, if a father enters into a contract to buy a car for his son and the seller refuses to deliver the vehicle after payment, the son cannot sue the seller for the delivery of the car. Only the father who has given consideration for the sale has that right.

Terms of Contract

When one party to a contract brings a court action against the other party, it is often on the ground that the latter has failed to fulfill his obligation under the contract. Now whether a party to a contract is under any contractual obligation depends on whether performance of that obligation is part of, or a term of, the contract.

1. Express

A term of contract is express if it is orally agreed upon by the parties at the time of concluding the contract or is contained in a written document embodying the contract.

2. Implied

A term may also be implied. It will be implied by conduct where even though they may not specifically have discussed it or agreed on it. They should, as reasonable people be taken to have intended that it should be part of the contract. For example, in a contract of employment, whether the parties specifically agreed on it or not, it will be implied that the employee should be paid his salary in full in any month if he is absent from work without permission or reasonable cause. Similarly, if it is customary in any industry that employees should receive a bonus at a certain point in time, that will be a term implied into their contracts of employment

Lastly, law implies a number of terms into specific contracts. For instance, it is an implied term in a contract for the sale of goods that the goods should fit for their intended use. Again, it is an implied term of a contract of employment that the employee should be entitled to a certain number of days every year as his annual leave

Conditions and Warranties

A term of contract (whether express or implied) may be a condition of the contract or a mere warranty, whether it is one or the other may depend on how it is called by the parties in their agreement. Generally, a condition is such an important term of contract that its breach by one party deprives the other of a substantial benefit of the contract so that he is entitled, if he so wishes, to regard himself as discharged from further performance of the contract. A warranty is a minor term so that its breach does not entitle the innocent party to consider himself discharged from further performance of the contract.

Discharge of a Contract

A party to a contract may be discharged (i.e., released) from further performance of the contract by the following factors.

1. **Mutual Agreement**
   This will happen where, after their agreement, they enter into a subsequent agreement whereby one of the parties is released from

his/her obligations under the contract. After the conclusion of that subsequent agreement, the party released will be discharged from further performance of the contract.

2. **Performance**

    A party to a contract may also be discharged by performance. For instance, where a contract is for the performance of specific tasks, once the party concerned completes that task, he has no further performance to render and the contract will automatically come to an end.

3. **Breach**

    As observed above, a breach by one party of a condition of the contract entitles the other party to regard himself as discharged from further performance of the contract. As a result, the latter can terminate the contract and proceed to recover any payment he may have made or any benefit he was supposed to get under the contract.

4. **Frustration**

    A party to a contract may also be discharged from further performance by frustration. This type of discharge occurs where a contract that was capable of performance at the time of its conclusion becomes incapable of performance because of subsequent developments.

These developments may be:

- subsequent illegality
- subsequent death of one of the parties
- Subsequent imprisonment of one of the parties for a substantial period of time and
- Subsequent cancellation of an expected event
- The effect of these developments will be to bring the contract to an end forthwith

Remedies

Where the court is satisfied that there has been a breach of contract, it has the power to grant the following remedies:

i.   Refusal of further performance by the innocent party. For example, if he has not yet paid the contract price, he can refuse to do so as a result of the party's breach;

ii. Damages as compensation for injury or loss suffered by the innocent party as a result of the breach;

iii. Quantum meruit, i.e. the value of the performance actually rendered by the innocent party.

iv. Specific performance. This remedy allows the innocent party to recover the performance promised by the party in breach and is generally not available except in cases involving land.

   Thus, for instance on a breach of the contract for the sale of goods, the court will rarely order the seller to deliver the goods agreed to be sold unless they are unique in some way. Usually in that case it will simply award the innocent party damages representing the value of the good.

   In a case where a seller of land fails or refuses to transfer the land to the buyer, the court will order the seller to do the transfer.

v.   **Injunction;**
   This is an order by the court stopping a contemplated or continuing breach of contract. Of course, this remedy is not final but interim. As a result, it is not uncommon to have an injunction vacated by the court on the application of the party against whom it is granted. Besides an injunction often tends to be for a fixed period of time and will lapse at the expiry of that period unless the court agrees to its extension.

Law of Agency

This is the relation which exists between two persons where one of them has authority or capacity to act on behalf of the other. In other words, agency relation arises whenever one person called the 'Agent' has authority to create legal obligations between the other called the *'principal' and third parties*. Thus, an Agent is only an intermediary between the other called the *'principal' and third parties*.

As a result, although he is bound to exercise his authority in accordance with all the lawful instructions of his principal, an Agent is not (unless he is also an employee of his principal) subject to the direct control or supervision of his principal in the performance of his duties.

Creation of the Agency Relation

The agency relation may be created by the express or implied agreement (which may be but does not need to be contractual) of the principal and the agent.

1. Express Agency

Express agency arises where the principal or some person authorized by him expressly (i.e. in writing or orally) appoints the agent to do either a specified number of things or to act for the principal generally.

2. Implied Agency

Implied agency will arise from the conduct or situation of the parties. And it is immaterial for this purpose that the third person had no authority in fact at the time to enter into that contract for the first person. This is called the doctrine of apparent authority or agency by estoppel

3. Agency by Ratification

Under some circumstances, an act which at the time when it was done lacked authority may by the subsequent conduct of the person on whose behalf lacked authority may by the subsequent conduct of the person on whose behalf lacked authority. For instance, if one person acts in such a way as to lead another person into believing that he has authorized a third person to act on his behalf and that other person in that belief enters into a contract with the third person. The third person will be an agent for the first person in respect of that contract.

This is because the first person is prevented from denying the fact that the person had no authority in fact the third person is his agent. Every act that is not void can be ratified so long as it is capable of ratification by the principal. The illegality of an act does not of itself prevents its ratification. Consequently, a principal may ratify a breach of contract and thus become liable for it

Ratification may be express or may be inferred in appropriate cases even from silence or mere acquiescence. Of course, in that latter case it must be based on the principal's full knowledge of all the essential facts of the act sought to be ratified and must relate to that particular act, and not some other transaction. As a result, the agent will be relieved of personal liability to his principal for acting in excess of his authority and to the third party for possible breach of warranty of authority.

Elements to be present in ratification

(a) The agent must not have been acting for himself in the first place but must have professed to be acting on behalf of a named or ascertainable principal

(b) The principal must have been in existence at the time of the action This is because a principal who was not in existence at the time when an act was purportedly done on his behalf cannot, on coming into existence, ratify the act

(c) The principal must have been capable of doing the act himself since a person cannot act as an agent for another person who has no capacity to act for himself

(d) The ratification must take place within the time fixed by the transaction itself or within a reasonable time thereafter

Agency by Necessity

The agency relation may also arise by necessity. This will be the case where by reason of an emergency, the relation of principal and agent is deemed to exist between persons who are not otherwise in such a relation. Agency of necessity exists between persons who are not otherwise in such a relation. An agency of necessity exists where to prevent destruction of perishable cargo, a carrier has to take prompt action in excess of his authority and dispose of it.

In other words, as a result of the emergency the agent has to extend his authority to save the principal's property from destruction. For an agency of necessity to arise:

a) The agent should not have been able to communicate with his principal on how to deal with the emergency
b) The action taken should have been necessary in the circumstance in that it was the only reasonable and prudent course open to the agent; and
c) The agent should have acted bona fide in the interests of the parties concerned

Acting in Principle's name

- But regardless of the type of authority involved since an agent derives his authority from his principal, he must act in the principal's name
- However, as will be shown below, the requirement is simply that he must disclose the principal's existence though he may not divulge the principal's identity

Agent's Capacity to Delegate

- An agent cannot delegate his authority except with the principal's express or implied assent
- As a result, in the absence of that assent, the principal will not be bound by the act or contract of a sub-agent whose appointment he has not sanctioned

Agent's Duties to His Principal

- ➤ to perform the act or business undertaken
- ➤ to exercise his discretion. Where the principal does not give him any definition instructions on any particular act or business, the agent must be guided by the honest exercise of his judgment and the principal's interests
- ➤ not to use any materials and information obtained by reason of the agency relation for his personal business
- ➤ to exercise reasonable care, diligence and skill of the principal
- ➤ to avoid any conflict between his interests and those of his principal
- ➤ not to make any secret profit from his position
- ➤ not to deny his principal's rights in an act done or transaction concluded on behalf of the principal

The Agent's Rights against His Principal

- To be paid the agreed remuneration. On the other hand, in the absence of any agreement on the matter, he has no right to be paid anything
- To be reimbursed and indemnified in respect of any expenses or liabilities incurred on behalf of the principal and in the exercise of his authority
- To exercise a right of lien on the principal's goods in respect of all claims against the principal arising out of the agency relation
- If he has bought goods on behalf of the principal with his own money or on credit' he stands towards the principal in the position of an unpaid seller

As a result, on delivery of the goods to a carrier for transmission to the principal, he can stop them in transit and resume possession

Principal's Relations with Third Parties

- Generally, the principal is bound by, and is entitled to the benefit of any contract made by his agent on his behalf within the scope of the agent's authority
- This is so whether at the time of acting the agent name or identified the principal or merely indicated that he was acting for a principal but did not identify him. i.e. the principal was disclosed.
- The rule also applies where the principal is undisclosed. i.e. where he is not known by the third party to be connected with the particular transaction, so long as in entering into the contract the agent clearly indicated that he was not acting on his own behalf.

The Agent's Relations with Third Parties

- A person who makes a contract in his own name without disclosing the existence of any principal is personally liable on the contract to the other contracting even though he may have been acting on behalf of the principal
- Similarly, if he claims to act on behalf of another person when the alleged principal does not exist, he will be personally liable for his act
- If he discloses the existence of the principal (ie. Where the principal, is disclosed but is unnamed) or both the existence and identity of the principal, he will not be subject to personal liability on the contract whether or not he had authority to make the contract
- Of course, where an agent purports to enter into a contract on behalf of a principal when he has no authority, he may be liable to the other party for the breach of warranty of authority unless the principal ratifies the contract
- As observed above, if the contract is ratified, that will have retrospective effect so that the agent's position will be as if he had

actual authority to conclude the contract on the principal's behalf when he did so

Termination of Agency

- Just like any other legal relationship between persons, the agency is terminable and that may happen by:

a) express revocation by the principal
b) renunciation by the agent
c) lapse of time. This will be the case where a specific period is fixed for the performance of the act to be done by the agent
d) performance i.e. where the agency was special, after the agent has performed the agreement act so that thereafter he becomes *functus officio*
e) by the death, bankruptcy or insanity of the principal; and the agent; and
f) any act that would generally amount to frustration

Sale of Goods

Contract of Sale of Goods

This is defined as a contract whereby one person (the seller) transfers or agrees to transfer the property in goods to another person (the buyer) for a money consideration called the price. Thus, from this definition it will be clear that the legal objective of the contract of sale of goods is for the buyer to obtain ownership of the goods while the seller receives their price in exchange.

The definition excludes any transaction intended to operate by way of mortgage, pledge, charge or other security. It does not apply to bailment, barter, contract of hire, hire-purchase and contracts for labour and materials. From the statutory definition, it is clear that the following elements must exist in a contract for it to amount to a contract of sale of goods

Buyer and Seller

The buyer is defined as a person who buys or agrees to sell goods. In other words, agreement is not a contract for the sale of goods unless the buyer is bound to buy the goods and the seller is to sell them to him. As a result, where there is a mere option to buy them as under the hire purchase) there will be no account for the sale of goods

Money Consideration

As definition of a contact of sale of goods it is clear that only contracts under which property in goods is transferred for money will be considered contracts for the sale of goods. On the other hand, a part –exchange transaction in which the agreed price is payable partly in money and

Goods. "Goods" refer to all movable property that is capable of transfer from one person to another by delivery. For the purposes of the contract of sale of goods, goods may be specific, ear marked (i.e. identified by the parties at the time of making the contract) and or unascertained, that is unidentified at the time of the contract and therefore requiring some subsequent agreed act of appropriation by the buyer or seller to earmark them to the contract

Property in Goods

As noted by definition, a contract for sale of goods involves the transfer of property in goods from the seller to the buyer. For this purpose, it would seem that the word "property" refers to the seller's absolute title to goods so that for a person to be able to sell goods under the contract of sale of goods, he must have a right of dominion over them

Form

- There are no legal formalities required for the conclusion of a valid sale of goods

a) Passing of Property

- When goods are transferred, the risk of loss or damage to the goods also passes from the seller to the buyer with the transfer of property
- Again, in the event of the seller becoming bankrupt or going into liquidation without having delivered specific goods, the buyer's right to claim possession of the goods from the seller's trustee in bankruptcy or liquidator will depend on whether property in the goods passed to the buyer before the commencement of the bankruptcy or liquidation
- In this case it will be useful to determine the point at which property in goods passes from the seller to the buyer

Specific Goods

Under the law, where there is a sale of specific goods, the property in them will pass to the buyer at such time as the parties intend it to be transferred. And to ascertain that intention, there must be regard to the terms of the contract, the conduct of the parties and the circumstances of the case. Obviously if the parties specifically agree on a particular event e.g. the payment of the price by the buyer or the delivery of the goods to the buyer, then the property will pass on the occurrence of either event.

However, where there is no such agreement or their conduct does not indicate any other intention, property in the goods will pass in accordance to the following rules:

Where the contract of sale is unconditional and the goods are in a deliverable state, property in them will pass to the buyer at the time when the contract is made. Where the seller is bound to do something to the goods to put them in deliverable state, property in them will not pass to the buyer until that is done and the buyer is aware that it has been done. Where the goods are in a deliverable state but the seller has to do something to them to ascertain their price (e.g.weigh, measure or test them) property in them will not pass until that is done and the buyer has noticed that it has been done

Uncertained Goods

Property in this type of goods will not pass until after they have been ascertained, i.e. after they have been unconditionally appropriated to the contract by the seller with the buyer's assent or by the buyer with the seller's assent

Passing of Risk

Legally the position is that, in the absence of agreement to the contrary by the party's goods remain at the seller's risk until the property in them is transferred to the buyer and once property passes to the buyer, the goods are at his risk even though they may not have been delivered to him

The word 'risk' is used here in connection with accidental loss or destruction of the goods. As a result, where goods are 'at the seller's risk' this means that if they are accidentally lost without fault on either side, being unable to deliver them to the buyer, the seller cannot recover their price already paid to him in advance.For the same reason, if they are at the buyer's risk and they get accidentally lost, he must pay the price even though he may not have taken possession of them as yet.

In other words, since the risk would be on the buyer, the loss would absolve the seller from his duty to deliver them and the buyer is obliged to accept delivery as if they conformed to the contract.

Transfer of Title

Although the contract of sale of goods is about transfer of property in them to the buyer, it sometimes becomes necessary to deal with the issue of transfer of title. And that question often arises where a non – owner sells the goods and the issue is to determine who, as between their real owner and the buyer is entitled to them.

And the general rule is *nemo dat quod non habet:* the transfer of goods cannot pass a better title than that he himself has. Essentially this means that a buyer of goods from a thief does not get title to them since his seller does not have title in the first place. However, this rule is subject to the following exceptions whose effect is that a person with no title to goods or who has no authority to sell them can pass a good title in them to a third party.

Where the non-owner is an agent of the real owner of the goods and has actual or apparent authority from the latter to sell them. Where the real owner has by his conduct held out the non-owner as being the real owner of the goods. Where the goods are sold on the open market the buyer acquires a good title to them provided he buys them in good faith. Where the seller has a voidable title (where he acquired the goods by misrepresentation, duress or under undue influence) but the title has not been avoided at the time of sale.

Where the goods are sold without the owner's consent by a person exercising statutory power the buyer will get a good title for them. Implied Obligations in favor of the Buyer. The law imposes a number of obligations on the seller:

- Conditions
- Warranties
- Where the buyer expressly or by implication discloses the purposes for which he requires the goods, it is an implied condition of the contract of sale that the goods will be reasonably suitable for that purpose
- Where there is a sale by sample, it is an implied condition of the contract of sale that the bulk will correspond with the sample in quality

Exclusion Clause

Of course, with the exception of the implied condition relating to the seller's right to sell, all the other implied conditions can be excluded by an appropriately worded clause. The clause must be clear and unambiguous and must be part of the contract of sale of goods.

Performance of the Sale of Goods

In the performance of the contract of sale of goods, the seller and the buyer are under the following mutual obligations:

1. Delivery of the goods to the buyer

    This is the seller's reciprocal duty to the buyer's obligations to accept the goods and pay for them. ***Generally, 'delivery' can be defined as the voluntary transfer of possession of goods from the seller to the buyer.***Of course, the seller need not physically take the goods to the buyer; it suffices if he makes them available for the buyer to collect them or arrange for their collection.

    In fact, as shown below in the majority of cases the seller delivers goods to the buyer without physically transferring them at all. Delivery may be actual as where the seller transfers physical possession to the buyer or the buyer's agent.

    Delivery may be 'constructive' and not involve any physical transfer of goods at all. Construct delivery may take any one of the following forms:

2. Transfer of a document of title
3. Delivery of an object giving physical control. The delivery to the buyer of keys to premises where the goods are stored is effective delivery of the goods to him
4. Continuous possession. If the buyer was already in possession of the goods as Bailee for the seller before making the contract of sale
5. Delivery to a carrier: where in terms of the contract of sale the seller is authorized or required to send the goods to the buyer, their delivery to the carrier for transmission to the buyer is effective delivery to the buyer

    If the property has already passed to the buyer at the time of rejection, the action may be for damages or for the price of the goods

Payment for the Goods

The buyer is obliged to pay for the goods in accordance with the terms of the contract of sale.

Remedies for Breach of Contract

Assuming that there has been breach of contract, the following remedies will be available to the parties.

a) Seller

If the property has passed to the buyer and he fails to pay for the goods, the seller can sue him for their price. If the seller is unpaid seller and he still has possession of the goods he can exercise the right of lien on them. The seller also has the right of stoppage of the goods. The unpaid seller also has right to resale the goods and recover from the proceeds of the unpaid price

b) The Buyer

For the buyer he has the following remedies:where the seller fails to comply with any one of the implied conditions, and the condition is not excluded the buyer can reject the goods and refuse to pay for them or recover the price he may have paid for them. As noted above where there is short or excessive delivery or the goods delivered are mixed with non – contract goods buyer is entitled to reject them.

Where the seller wrongfully neglects or refuses to deliver the goods, the buyer is entitled to sue him for breach of contract and recover as damages the estimated loss resulting from that breach. In the case of the seller's wrongful neglect or refusal to deliver the goods the buyer may also be entitled to specific performance

Where the seller is in breach of warranty, or an implied condition but the buyer has accepted the goods so that the breach of condition can only be treated as a breach of warranty, the buyer is entitled to sue him for damages representing the loss resulting from that breach. It should be noted that in the absence of any agreement to the contrary where the buyer refuses to accept goods delivered to him under circumstances where he is entitled to refuse delivery he is not bound to return them to the seller. It suffices to simply intimate to the seller that he refuses to accept them.

Government Regulation

Although most Entrepreneurs recognize the need for some government regulation of business, most believe the process is overwhelming and out of control. Government regulation of business is far from new. To date laws regulating business practices and government agencies to enforce the regulations have expanded continuously. Most Entrepreneurs agree that some government regulation are necessary. There must be laws governing working safety, environmental protection, package labeling, consumer credit and other relevant issues because some dishonest, unscrupulous managers will abuse the opportunity to serve the public interest. It is not the regulations that protect workers and consumers and achieve social objectives that businesses object to, but those that produce only marginal benefits relative to their costs. Entrepreneurs especially seek relief from wasteful and meaningless government regulations, charging that the cost of compliance exceeds the benefits gained.

All businesses, regardless of type, must comply with statutes (laws passed by legislative bodies) and regulations (rules enacted by regulatory agencies to carry out the purposes of statutes). These statutes and regulations can come from all levels of government; federal, state, and local. Some of these statutes and regulations apply regardless of the nature of the business and, of course, a venture engaged in business in more than one state or local jurisdiction must comply with applicable laws and regulations from all applicable jurisdictions.

The enforcement agency has no obligation to notify the business that it must comply with the law. It is the business's obligation to inquire and comply. Fortunately, most agencies have public information departments eager to assist in providing information and obtaining compliance. These laws and regulations include licensing and registration of business name, workers compensation, unemployment compensation, and permission to do business in a form other than a sole proprietorship. The collection of sales taxes and the withholding of employees' wages are further examples of obligations with which to comply.

PART II

CRAVE FOR PRINCIPLES
OF SUCCESS

CHAPTER 10

Take Business as a Calling

Taking Business as a calling simply means doing what you were born to do. This could be a process of discovering your purpose by reading books, listening to tapes, watching videos and attending seminars – studying successful people and establishing why and how they succeed. In pursuit of this you may learn that those who succeed are no better qualified than yourself.

You may be shocked to discover that you are capable of doing things that you never knew you are capable of doing. The key to life is discovery of a clear personal purpose and a sense of destiny and a vision that motivates.

Colossians 4:17 says:'Say to Achipus, take heed to the ministry which thou received in the Lord that thou fulfill it.' From this scripture, it shows that *failure to identify yourself with your purpose could lead you to invest in wrong areas of investments and that can lead to frustration.* Taking business as a calling starts with beginning with the right environment. Just as each of us has a unique figure print, you are also born with a unique purpose that only you can fulfill.

Start creating the environment for your purpose to be developed, matured and revealed to mankind. It is worth noting the words of Emile Bissel, "Great thoughts speak only to the thought mind, but great actions speak to all mankind." In many cases, you will grow through a period of soul searching before your purpose will be revealed to you.

Wherefore the rather brethren give diligence to make your calling and election sure for if ye do these things ye shall never fail. 2 Peter 1:10 And with the realization that you can identify that a baby is a human being, but cannot know what it will become one day, you will know when you have found your purpose, but will not know how it will be fulfilled. *Commit your works to the Lord and your plans will be established (Proverbs 16:30.* The how will always come later. The most important thing right now is to have a dream which you need to commit to God to effect the delivery.

The mind of man plans his way, but the Lord directs his steps. Proverbs 16:9. Your great business is inched in discovering your purpose which is directly linked with your talents, skills and abilities. ***Your purpose or calling is eagerly waiting for the right environment to generate and reveal itself to the world.*** This is a call to join the dreamers' world. Allow yourself to imagine and fantasize about the kind of business and life you would like to have. Think about the money you would like to earn as a return on your investment. You may wish to know that great men and women begin with a dream of something wonderful and different from what they have today.

Brian Tracy calls this practice "back from the future" thinking. This is a powerful technique practiced continually by high performing men and women. This way of thinking has an amazing effect on your mind and on your behavior. Here is how it works: Project yourself forward five years. Imagine that five years have passed and that your life is now perfect in every respect.

What does it look like? What are you doing? How much money are you having in the bank? What kind of life do you have? Create a vision for yourself for the long - term future. The clearer your vision of healthy, happiness and prosperity, the faster you move toward it and the faster it moves toward you. **Where there is no vision, the people perish: but he that keepeth the law, happy is he (Proverbs 29:18).** When you a create mental picture of where you are going in life, you become more positive, more motivated and more determined to make it a reality. You trigger your natural creativity and come up with idea after idea to help make your vision come true.

You always tend to move in the direction of your dominant dreams, images and visions. The very act of allowing yourself to dream big dreams actually raises your self-esteem and causes you to like and respect yourself more. This in return improves your self – concept and increases your level of self-confidence. It also increases your personal level of self-respect and happiness.

CHAPTER 11

Craft Clear Strategic Vision

God has a plan for everyone including you. *"For I know the plans I have for you, says the Lord. They are plans for good and not for evil, to give you a future and a hope.."*.(Jeremiah 29:11)

You are not created to roam about in life purposelessly. You are designed for a specific placement. Before you were born, He knew you and separated you for a specific goal and assignment. To be a visionary you have to see ahead. Yes you need to have long term view. You have to see around the corners. This means you have to believe in things that no one else really believe.

But your placement in the grand master plan of God is located by vision. Strategic Vision is a description of the Road Map having three key questions: Where are we? Where do we want to be? How do we get there? Therefore, your views and conclusions about the business's long term direction is what constitute a strategic vision.

Vision therefore, is the source and hope of life and the greatest gift ever given to mankind. Sight is not at a level of vision. Sight is a function of the eyes; vision is a function of the heart. Eyes that look are common, but eyes that see are rare. No invention, development, or great feat was ever accomplished without the inspiring power of this mysterious source called vision.

Contrary to what some believe, vision is not that dream one has in the night. A true vision is the unfolding of divine plan and purpose. Everyone is created to fulfill a purpose on earth, just as every manufacturer creates a product specifically to fulfill a purpose. Therefore, a discovery of the purpose for which you are created is called vision. It is the unfolding of divine plan as it relates to a nation, a group or an individual.

Vision makes suffering and disappointment bearable. Vision generates hope in the midst of despair and provides endurance in tribulation. Vision inspires the depressed and motivates the discouraged. Without vision, life would be a study in cyclic frustration within a whirlwind of despair.

Then there are those who had a vision but have abandoned it because of discouragement, some measure of failure or frustration. If you are in one of these categories the Power of Vision is designed to help you understand the nature of vision, define a vision, capture or recapture a personal vision, simplify your vision and document your vision.

You were born to achieve something significant, and you were destined to make a difference in your generation. Your life is not a divine experiment but a project of providence to fulfill the purpose that your generation needs. This personal purpose is the source of your vision and gives meaning to your life.

Your vision is not ahead of you but it lies within you. Start seeing beyond eyes and live for the unseen. It is your vision that determines your destiny. Dr. David Oyedepo in his Book "In pursuit of vision" he says that, 'Knowing that it is yours but not knowing how to get at it can be frustrating.'

Our world today is in desperate need of vision. ***Prov 29:18 says, "Where there is no vision, the people perish"***. These words have been quoted and repeated by millions of people over the years. The full essence of his (Solomon) statement implies that where there is no revelation of the future, people perish. There are many who have no vision for their lives and wonder how to obtain one. There are others who have a vision, but are stuck in the mud of confusion not knowing what to do next.

There is no escaping the need for a strategic vision. Armed with a clear well-conceived business course for your business to follow, managers have a beacon to guide resource allocation and a basis for crafting a strategy to get the company where it needs to go. Businesses whose managers neglect the task of thinking strategically about the company's future business path are prone to drift aimlessly and lose any claim to being an industry leader. A business's mission statement is typically focused on its present business scope: "who we are and what we do". For you and everyone to perform at highest level require a mission.

Mission Statements broadly describe business's present capabilities, customer focus, activities and business make up. Establishing mission statement based on core values is equivalent to digging a foundation to your building.

The difference between strategic vision and mission statement is that a mission statement speaks to what a company is doing today while strategic vision generally has much greater direction – setting and strategy – making value Mission Statement has two questions: In what business are we in? and why are we in business.

The question why are we in business leads to objectives of the business. Business objectives involve converting the strategic vision into specific performance outcomes for the company to achieve. The purpose of setting objectives is to convert managerial statements of strategic vision and business mission into specific performance targets – results and outcomes the organization wants to achieve.

Setting Objectives and then measuring whether they are achieved or not help managers track an organization's progress. Managers of the best performing companies tend to set objectives that require stretch and disciplined effort. The challenge of trying to achieve bold, aggressive performance targets pushes an organization to be more inventive, to exhibit some urgency in improving both its financial performance (financial objectives) and business position (strategic objectives) and to be more intentional.

CHAPTER 12

Plan for Success

This is a true saying, "walk behind your success". This means that you implement the right step at the right time. Do not start big since everything that is big begins small. Do not rent an expensive office or space. Ensure that you do not employ expensive staff and avoid overstretching yourself. It is great to think big but you need time to action your big plans. Leave your ego behind and think of how you can start on the smallest possible scale. It is easy to learn and make mistakes when you are small.

The most successful entrepreneurs didn't start with a rigid business plan or funding but they ended up growing a massive business you can learn their secrets and succeed like them. No business is an island. A successful wealthy entrepreneur is dependent on an entrepreneur behind it but more importantly the relationships he or she has with others. This is what I call networking. This now takes us to the need for understanding strategic planning.

Strategic Planning deals with strategic management which is a stream of decisions and actions that leads to the development of an effective strategy or strategies to help achieve corporate objectives. Strategic Planning is the way in which successful people formulate and implement strategies.

Strategic Planning is concerned with deciding on a strategy and planning how that strategy is to be put into effect. Peter Drucker states that the task of thinking through the mission of the business, that is asking the question, what is my calling and what should my assignment be? Is critical to the school of vision and strategic planning. This leads to the setting of objectives, the development of strategies, strategy implementation and evaluation and controls.

There's this guy who dreams of living in a nice house. He imagines the house in great detail. Where it will be, how it will look, what it will have, who will live in it – everything. Sadly, far too many people delay their own success because they lack an ACTION PLAN. They dream of success, but without action, they cannot experience the success they want so ba

I had a plan. I had a purpose for my success. I had a vision. Do you? If you don't, get to work on it - right now! One of the best issues I remember is about creating your own business plan. When I followed it, and drafted out my own plan, I noticed improved results within a year – and they have never stopped getting better.

Choose Success

Imagine driving in a car to a place you want to go, and the road gets bumpy. What do you do? You could stop, get out of the car, and curse your bad luck. You could turn your car around and go back to the smooth, quiet road to nowhere.

Or…

You could keep going on, determined to get where you are going – and knowing things will get better when you reach there. Not just keep going, but actually ENJOY the ride. And even be thankful that you have got a car, and that you know the way!

Every Dream Will Be Tested!

Anything worth getting is worth working hard to get - and worth waiting for. If it is so quick and easy to achieve that anyone can get it, is it really going to be very desirable? Think of the things you – and most other people – want, dream about, strive for. Are they things ANYONE can get – quickly, easily?"Far better to dare mighty things, to win glorious triumphs, even though checkered by failure, than to take rank with those poor spirits who neither enjoy much nor suffer much, because they live in the gray twilight that knows not victory, nor defeat."

So, decide you are going to succeed – no matter what. It could take a long time. It could involve hard work. It could mean putting up with temporary discomfort.

Keep Learning For Success

One of the critical elements I identified in becoming successful is learning. Constant, ongoing education. As you keep learning, you keep growing. Stop – and you cease to grow. I have always invested in my education – at first, with my time (reading free material), and later, money.

Risky? Yes, it was – to me, at that point in time.

Still, I took the risk. And did it because of the potential benefits. It paid off. In less than a year, I have got back multiples of my investment – and can do many times better with this profit than I could before.

Learn From Success

While learning is important, learning from the right person is even more important. Choose your teachers wisely, carefully. Following the wrong guide can be more harmful than not learning at all!

The lessons you will learn, the life experiences you will gain, the attitudes and approaches you will develop on your way to the top will be more important in defining your 'success' than any material reward you may receive.

Model Success

Find someone who you think is a success. Learn from his or her approach and strategy. Watch everything they do. Read everything they write. Listen to everything they say. And think about it. Analyze it. Try it out and test it. Pretty soon, something amazing happens – you will see similar success in your business, your marketing, your life.

And it is not just people. If you see a successful sales letter, model it on your sales page. If someone uses a successful marketing approach, model it in your own marketing. If you come across an exciting or innovative strategy that is also successful, try it out in your own business.

If you are working online, this is pretty difficult to do – unless you network actively. I'm not a very outgoing or sociable person. I suspect most

Internet marketers are not – otherwise, they'd be marketing in person, not on the Net!

Still, despite all the 'advantages' of anonymity and 'work at home' convenience, it is important to go out and meet and interact with others. *No great things were ever achieved alone and in insecurity. You always need others to help you – if you want to be a success.*

Enjoy Success

Far too many people chase an elusive 'Success' – and never find it. Worse, they get frustrated, stressed out, unhappy in the aimless quest. To enjoy success, you must appreciate it. Be grateful for what you have. Cherish and respect it. All too often, we complain about things we do not have – and forget everything we have. One of my most powerful 'Success Secrets' is to delight in what I already have. It helps to have constant reminders of these facts in my daily life, where I work with unfortunate children born with life-threatening heart problems.

CHAPTER 13

Understanding Business Ethics

Many Business Commentators say that business ethics is critical and is a structured examination of how people and institutions should behave in the world of commerce. In particular, it involves examining appropriate constraints on the pursuit of self-interest, or (for firms) profits, when the actions of individuals or firms affect others. At the heart of business ethics is rightness or wrongness. For example, is it morally right to engage in insider trading? Is it morally correct to be involved in corporate lies? However, many business commentators say that business ethics is the discipline of applying general ethical dilemmas in business dealings.

The rule of the game is that you need to be smart. Never use shortcut suicide. As professional entrepreneur ensure that you are not involved in anything illegal. In simple terms do not indulge yourself in anything that is ethically questionable.

According to Chris (2009) *"BUSINESS ETHICS" is the study of ethical dilemmas, values, and decision-making in the world of commerce.* It applies to all aspects of business conduct and is relevant to the conduct of individuals and business organizations as a whole. Business ethics (also known as Corporate ethics) is a form of professional ethics that examines ethical principles and moral or ethical problems that arise in a business environment.

Applied ethics is a field of ethics that deals with ethical questions in many fields such as medical, technical, legal and business ethics. Business ethics can be both a normative and a descriptive discipline. As a corporate practice and a career specialization, the field is primarily normative. In academia descriptive approaches are also taken. The range and quantity of business ethical issues reflects the degree to which business is perceived to be at odds with non-economic social values.

Business ethics and the changing Environment

Businesses and governments operate in changing technological, legal, economic, social and political environments with competing stakeholders and power claims. Stakeholders are individuals, companies, groups and nations that cause and respond to: external issues, opportunities and threats. Internet and information technologies, globalization, deregulation, mergers and wars, have accelerated rate of change and uncertainty.

In today's dynamic and complex environment stakeholders such as professionals, shareholders, management, employees, consumers, suppliers and members of community must make and manage business and moral decisions.

Environmental Forces and Stakeholders Organizations are embedded in and interact with multiple changing local, national and international environments. These environments are increasingly moving toward and emerging into a global system of dynamically interrelated interactions among local, national and international.

A first step toward understanding stakeholder issues is to gain an understanding of environmental forces that influence issues and stakes of different groups. This is a call to think globally before acting locally in many situations. As we discuss an overview of these environmental forces here, think of the effects and pressures each of the forces has on your industry, company, profession or career and job.

Stakeholder Management Approach

The question is: how do companies, communication media, political groups, consumers, employees, competitors and other groups respond when they are affected by an issue, dilemma, threat or opportunity from one or more of the environments described? The stakeholder management approach is a way of understanding the effects of environmental forces and groups on specific issues that affect real – time stakeholders and their welfare.

The stakeholder approach begins to address these questions by enabling individuals and groups to articulate collaborative, win – win strategies.

The underlying aim here is to develop awareness of the ethics and social responsibility of different stakeholders' perceptions, plans, strategies and actions.

Business Ethics: Why Does It Matter?

Business ethicists ask, "What is right and wrong, good and bad, and harmful and beneficial regarding decisions and actions in and around organizational activities? Ethical "solutions" to business and organizational problems may seem available. Thus, learning to think, reason and act ethically can enable us to first be aware and recognize a potential problem.

"Doing the right thing" matters to all stakeholders.

To companies and employers, acting legally and ethically means saving billions of dollars each year in lawsuits, settlements and theft. Studies have also shown that corporations also have paid significant financial penalties for acting unethically. ***Costs to businesses also include: deterioration of relationships; damage to reputation; declining employee productivity; loyalty and absenteeism; companies that have a reputation of unethical and uncaring behavior toward employees also have a difficult time recruiting and retaining valued professional.***

For business leaders and managers, managing ethically also means managing with integrity. Integrity cascades throughout an organization. It shapes and influences the values, tone and culture of the organization, commitment and imagination of everyone in a company. Then, we can evaluate our own and other's values, assumptions and judgments regarding the problem before we act.

Laura Nash points out that business ethics deals with three basic areas of managerial decisions making. First, is a choice about what the laws should be and whether to follow them. Second, choices about economic and social issues outside the domain of law, and lastly, choices about the priority of self – interest over the company's interest.

What Are Unethical Business Practices? Surveys identify prominent everyday ethical issues facing businesses and their stakeholders. Recurring themes include: managers lying to employees or vice versa; office favoritism;

taking credit for others' work; receiving or offering kickbacks; stealing from the company; firing an employee for whistle-blowing. padding expenses accounts to obtain reimbursements for questionable business expenses; divulging confidential information or trade secrets commonly called insider trading; terminating employment without giving sufficient notice and using company property and materials for personal use.

Things That Ethics Promotes

- Openness and transparency
- Honesty and integrity
- Excellence and quality
- Public accountability
- Legality
- Promote justice
- Confidential information
- Balanced decisions
- Whistle blowing

Relativism

Although relativism is most often associated with ethics, one can find defenses of relativism in virtually any area of philosophy. Both relativism and morality involve the field of ethics, also called moral philosophy, which involves systematic, defending and recommending concepts of right and wrong behavior. ***The term ethics is also defined as a discipline involving inquiry into more judgments people make and the rules and principles upon which such judgments are based.***

There are two different versions of relativism: Factual Moral Relativism (FMR) and Normative Ethical Relativism (NER) as it is often claimed that moral beliefs are in fact relative. It will be useful to generalize a distinction familiar from discussions of ethical relativism and to distinguish FMR and NER with respect to anything that is claimed to be relative.

Moral beliefs are in fact relative, that different people do make different moral judgments and advocates different more rules and principles.

Thus, FMR claims that moral ideals and the like are often countered by arguments that such things are universal. Therefore, FMR are empirical claims that may tempt us to conclude that they are little philosophical interests, but there are several reasons why this is so.

This position is called FMR and as factual matter, the truth of FMR can be decided by empirical investigation. On the other hand, Normative Ethical Relativism (NER) is a claim that an Act in Society S is right if and only if most people in society S believe A is right. This is a Universal Normative Principal in so far as it applies to any person in society.

However, the possibility of NER arises only when some action or practice is the focus of disagreement between holders of two self-contained and exclusive systems. For example, two systems of beliefs, S1 and S2, are exclusive of one another when they have consequences that disagree under some description but do not require either to abandon their side of the disagreement.

Thus, a real confrontation between S1 and S2 would occur when S2 is real option for the group living under S1. From the forgoing discussion we can conclude that NER seems to be a less powerful tool not robust enough and less convincing since in both society S1 and fails to understand why the same tool is interpreted differently.

However, it is argued that if the principal of tolerance is accepted the society groups need not impose nor foster tolerance on moral beliefs on others. On such, NER can be accepted because it is the only normative principal with commitment to tolerance. To their concepts, beliefs or modes of reasoning, then groups cannot differ with respect to their concepts, beliefs or modes of reasoning.

Further, the NER supported by FMR takes on a more practical task, which is to arrive on one hand. FMR does not necessarily deny the existence of a single correct moral appraisal, given the same set of circumstances. This means that FMR as a tool for supporting NER with empirical investigation NER in a given area tends to counsel tolerance of practices that conform to alternatives standards prevailing in the area. FMR input into NER claims that different cultures have different views of morality, which they unify under one general conception of morality.

FMR presupposes some measure of realism. For example, if there are no such things as concepts, beliefs or modes of reasoning, then groups cannot differ with respect at more standards that regulate right and wrong conduct. Thus, this may involve articulating the good habit that we should acquire, the duties that we should follow in consequences of our behavior on others.

Ethical Theory

COGNITIVISM AND NON-COGNITIVISM

The first and most profound division in ethical theory is between the claim that it is possible to know moral right from wrong and denial of that claim. Because this is claim and encounter-claim about what we can and cannot know, the position which declares we can know is called 'cognitivism' and the contrary position 'non-cognitivism.'

According to cognitivism, there are objective moral truths which can be known, just as we can know other truths about the world. Statements of moral belief, on this view can be true or false just as our statement that something is a certain colour can be true or false. According to the non-cognitivist, by contrast, 'objective' assessment of moral belief is not possible. It is all 'subjective'.

There is no truth or falsity to be discovered. There is only belief, attitude, emotional reaction, and the like. As Hamlet puts it, 'There is nothing either good or bad but thinking makes it so'. When non-cognitivism claims that there are only attitudes, its proponents do not usually mean that moral judgments are simply expressions of one's feelings. Advocates of non-cognitivism acknowledge the essentially social nature of morality by invariably arguing that these are group attitudes.

Consequentialism versus Non-Consequentialism

The greatest divide in cognitivist thinking is between theories which assess moral right and wrong in terms of the consequences of actions and those which do not. Those which do are 'consequentialist' theories; those which do not are 'non-consequentialist'. With consequentialist theories, we look to the results of actions to determine the truth or falsity of moral judgments about them. If what follows from an action is, on balance, of benefit then it is, a good action and so we are right to do it. Conversely, if the outcome is, on balance harmful then the action is 'bad' and we are 'wrong' to do it. For consequentialism, the test of whether an action is right or wrong is whether it is good or bad in the sense of resulting in benefit or harm.

In this case right or wrong is a question of good or bad; and good or bad a question of benefit or harm. For non-consequentialism, there is no immediate appeal to beneficial or harmful consequences to determine good or bad. Divine Command theory offers an illustration of the difference between consequentialism and non-consequentialism. If religious believers were to obey God's commands in order to attain a desirable state after death, or because they believed that obedience was rewarded by material success, then such moves presuppose a consequentialist view of ethic.

If, however, the believer obeys God's commands, not for any expected reward, but for the sole reason that God has commanded them, then he or she presupposes a strictly non-consequentialist account of morality. It is not what follows from our actions which then make them right or wrong but only the fact of their conformity or non-conformity to God's commands.

It is solely in virtue of being activities of such a conforming or non-conforming kind that actions are right or wrong and therefore good or bad. Taken item by item, a consequentialist and non-consequentialist listing of rights and wrongs will probably not differ very much. Of course, there will be some disagreement on substantive moral issues and they are, unsurprisingly, likely to concern just those issues that divide society the most.

Utilitariasm: An ethical of welfare

The best-known consequentialist theory of ethics is called 'utilitarianism'. The name derives from the use of the word utility to denote the capacity in actions to have good results. This choice of word proclaims the consequentialist nature of the theory. Utility means usefulness – under lying the point that it is the usefulness of actions which determines their moral character than anything in the nature of the action itself.

Actions are not good or bad in themselves, but only in what they are good or bad for. Although, strictly speaking, good and bad are the results, while utility and disutility are the capacities for those results, they amount to the same thing in practice and can, for convenience, be treated as synonymous.

CHAPTER 14

Let the Figures Make Noise

Business and money are practically one in the same. How much should you charge for your goods or services? Should you extend credit? How do you go about accepting credit cards? Whatever the issue, understanding the financial aspect of business is vital.

Making a Profit

Just how important is selecting the right price? It could mean the difference between success and failure. One of the most important financial concepts you will need to learn in your new business is the computation of profit and how it relates to your pricing structure. The gross profit on a product sold or service rendered is computed as the money you brought in from the sale, less the cost of the goods sold. The key is to compute accurately the cost of goods sold, which can be deceptive.

Pricing Your Goods or Service

It should be clear by now that the wrong price can put you out of business fast. Finding that magic number requires careful thought and planning. The trick is to come up with a price that gives you a good profit while still attracting customers. When first opening their doors, many businesspeople have a hard time knowing what to charge for their product or service. But actually, it is not that hard to figure out. If you sell a product, you base your retail price on your wholesale cost. The real trick is figuring out what to charge when you have a service business.

Cheaper Isn't Always Better. It is equally important to understand that being the cheapest is not always smart. When you use price as the only barometer for your services, then other more important things get left out of the equation—like quality, personal service, and promptness. McDonald's can emphasize low prices because that is one of its trademarks.

But if you are not a McDonald's-type outfit, constantly discounting fees and prices may be a mistake. ***The price of a product tells consumers what kind of value and quality to expect before they buy it.*** A person who can afford a Mercedes or Jaguar doesnot mind the high price because they associate quality and value with the prices of these cars.

Often, in a consumer's mind, the higher price, the higher the quality, and a low price means poor quality. You need to ask yourself whether you are trying to increase profit margins or market share. If you are mostly interested in boosting profits rapidly.

Let the Figures Do the Talking If you donot understand the finances of business, and many Entrepreneurs actually do not, you are in trouble. Business decisions that are not based, at least in part, on a cold and hard financial analysis are decisions that can easily go wrong. For example, assume that your business is looking to add a new product line. How do you know if it will work? Such an important decision should not be based on guesswork or hunches.

Instead, you have to let the figures do the talking. Knowing how to crunch the numbers—figuring out what it will cost you to launch the new line, how much you can expect to make, and how quickly you can reasonably expect to make it—will make the decision easy for you. Can you afford a new product line? Will your cash flow allow you to afford it? What kind of return on this investment of capital and time can you expect? Let the figures do the talking.

That is what Starbucks does. How does Starbucks know when to open up another store in a neighborhood? They look at existing stores and notice how long customers have to wait to have their order taken and filled and then open another in that area when the wait gets too long. They let the figures do the talking. That is what you must do. Can you afford that new product line? Well, what do the numbers say? If the numbers are not there, your brainstorm could be a huge mistake.

And if you don't know what the numbers are saying, it is time to learn. Supply and demand for the product you are producing. It has to be done with testing and care. The second way to increase your gross profit margin is to lower your costs. Decreasing the costs of materials or producing the product more efficiently can accomplish this. Look for a less costly supplier.

Whether you are starting a service business, a manufacturing outfit, a wholesaling venture, or a retail store, you should always strive to deliver your product or service more efficiently, with less cost, and at a price that gives you the best profit. The name of the game is, after all, making a profit.

Your Customers' Payment Options

The final financial aspect you need to deal with at this point has to do with what forms of payment to accept. This includes the creation of a credit policy and the decision of whether to accept checks and credit cards.

There are two important aspects to a successful customer credit policy. First, limit you risk. Second, investigate each customer's creditworthiness. Once a potential customer has completed the application, you need to verify the facts and assess the company's creditworthiness. You do so by calling references and by using a credit reporting agency or business consulting firms. Finally, even if the client seems worthy, and even if he or she checks out, trust your gut.

Chapter 15

Improve on Stakeholder Management Skills

What Stakeholder Management is all About?

Stakeholder management deals with managing all those that have an interest in our business. I call them parents to the organization. These parents include but not limited to employees or staff, management, shareholders, customers, suppliers, lenders of finance and competitors. Managing the aforementioned stakeholders will lead to the success of the business. For the sake of you the reader of this book I have presented part of these stakeholders for you to appreciate the impact they have on the business. Let us now look at the stakeholders one by one.

How to Manage a Customer

As already pointed out a customer is one of the stakeholders. Failure to mange customers could lead to low sales or no sales. This can give risk to the futurity of the business. To this end it is important that an entrepreneur should seek to meet the expectations of his or her customers, should seek to delight the expectations of his or her customers and more importantly the entrepreneur must amaze his or her customers. In pursuit of managing a customer the first logical step is to analyze customers. Customer analysis starts with segmentation. This looks at asking the following questions:

- Who are the biggest customers?
- The most profitable customers
- The most attractive potential customers

- Do the customers fall into any logical groups on the base of needs, motivations or characteristics?
- How should the market be segmented into groups that would require a unique business strategy?

The second strategy in managing a customer revolves around understanding customer behavior. This looks at questions such as:

- Why do customers select and use their favorite brands?
- What elements of the product/service do they value most?
- What are the customers' objectives?
- What are they really buying?
- What changes are occurring in customer motivation?
- What motivates them to go to supplier x or y?
- Customer analysis is trying to be close as possible to them to know what motivates them to go to supplier x

As an entrepreneur you need to convince them that they have been going to wrong products but they should have come to you. It is up to you to convince them that our product, price, place (channels of distribution) and promotional methods will be able to bring solutions to their problems. The idea is feedback and making sure that they always comeback (Customer Relationship Marketing). Always be ahead of customers with new ideas (4Ps).

How to Manage a Supplier

The art of managing a supplier is vital to the success of an enterprise. For instance, suppliers provide raw materials, goods or services required by an organization in order to function. Suppliers can therefore help or hurt, build or break an organization depending on their ability to provide needed materials at the right time. On its part the supply of labour has a lot of bearing on the success of an organization. Availability of quality and skilled labour tends to determine the past, present and future shape of a firm.

Markets exist because of the interaction of two forces, supply and demand. We then bring the two together in order to get complete picture and understanding of the markets. This is the basis upon economists explain price determination. In our case we are interested in how and why markets work and the interaction of customers and potential suppliers.

Suppliers can affect an industry through their ability to raise prices or reduce the quality of purchased goods and services. A supplier or a group of suppliers is powerful if some of the following factors apply: The supplier industry is dominated by a few companies, but it sells to many, e.g. the petroleum industry. Its commodity is unique and/or it has build up switching costs.

Substitutes are not readily available. Suppliers are able to integrate forward and compete directly with their present customers. Customers buy a small proportion of the supplier's product. The above factors are what are known as micro-factors of environmental influences. On the other hand we have what we call the macro-factors. These macro-factors (also called the social environment) are variables within a corporation's social environment.

They are the general forces that do not directly touch on the short-run activities of the organization but that can, and often do, influence its long-run decisions. These include the following: economic forces that regulate the exchange of materials; money; energy; and information; technological forces that generate problem solving inventions; political-legal forces that allocate power and provide constraining and protecting laws and regulations; sociocultural forces that regulate the values, mores and customs of society.

Managing Competitors

Considering competition is another important aspect organizations need to consider seriously. The competitive environment includes such factors as how the firm rates in the market share, technological innovation, financial strength, involvement in growth industries and the development of its human resources. A firm might be financially sound, have good personnel and dominate its industry, yet if the company is positioned in a declining industry, management may have to take aggressive action to move it to new expanding markets.

One important point to note is that competitive environment is not static, instead it is dynamic and sometimes it could be complex and in some instances it could be volatile. In most industries, corporations are mutually dependent. A competitive move by one firm can be expected to have a noticeable effect on its competitors and thus may cause retaliation or counter-efforts.

Intense rivalry is related to the presence of several factors, including: Number of competitors. When competitors are few and roughly equal in size, they watch each other carefully to make sure that any move by another firm is matched by an equal countermove. Rate of industry growth. For example, any showing in passenger traffic tends to set off price wars in the airline industry because the only path to grow is to take sales away from a competitor.

Amount of fixed costs is another area. For example, because airlines must fly their planes on a schedule regardless of the number of paying passengers for any one flight, they offer cheap standby fares whenever a plane has empty seats. If the only way a manufacturer can increase capacity is in a large increment by building a new plant, it will run that new plant at full capacity to keep its unit costs as low as possible – thus producing so much that the selling price falls throughout the industry.

Rivals that have very different ideas of how to compete are likely to cross paths often and unknowingly challenge each other's position. Sometimes they could be what we call threat of substitutes. Substitute products are those products that appear to be different but can satisfy the same needs as another product. For instance, in Malawi, coffee is a substitute for tea. Substitutes limit the potential returns of an industry by placing a ceiling on the prices firms in the industry can profitably charge.

If the price of coffee goes up high enough, coffee drinkers will slowly begin switching to tea. The price goes up high enough, coffee drinkers will slowly begin switching to tea. The price of tea thus puts a price ceiling on the price of coffee.

New entrants to an industry typically bring to its new capacity, a desire to gain market share, and substantial resources. They are, therefore, threats to an established cooperation. The threat of entry depends on the presence of entry barriers and the reaction that can be expected from existing competitors. An entry barrier is an obstruction that makes it difficult for a company to enter an industry.

Some of the possible barriers to entry are: economies of scale. Economies of scale occur when a firm grows in size and experience reduction in costs as a result of increasing production. Product differentiation. These are the differences in the production or appearances of a product. Sometimes it can occur through high levels of advertising and promotion. Capital requirements. This occurs when an existing firm has huge financial resources to create a significant barrier to entry to any competitor.

Managing Lenders of Finance

Lenders of finance are suppliers of finance or money. This is part of financial management. Financial management is that branch of management accounting which deals with the management of finances in order to achieve the financial objectives of an organization. It deals with the acquisition and allocation of resources among firms, the firm's present and potential activities and projects" Acquisition is concerned with the "financial decision", the generation of funds internally or externally at lowest possible cost. Allocation is concerned with the "investment decision", the use of these funds to achieve corporate financial objectives.

The conventional assumption is that most trading organizations' objective is the maximization of the value of the company for its owners. Since the owners of a company are its shareholders or an entrepreneur, the primary objective of a trading company is said to be "the maximization of shareholders' or an entrepreneurs wealth.

It must be emphasized though that while businesses do have to consider other stakeholders, from a corporate finance perspective, such objectives should only consider other stakeholders, from a corporate finance perspective, such objectives should only be pursued in support of the overriding long-term objective of maximizing shareholders' wealth. Modern finance theory usually assumes that the objective of the firm is to maximize the wealth of shareholders or entrepreneur.

Other possible objectives of the business include: Maximizing Profits Market Share, Obtaining Greater "Managerial Power", Increasing Employee Welfare, Increasing Social Responsibility, and Corporate

Growth. These objectives are operative but tend to be less important than maximizing shareholders' or entrepreneur's wealth.

Lenders of Finance are also called financial institutions. These are financial intermediaries that accept deposits from savers and invest in capital markets. Their functions range from accepting deposits, payment mechanism, borrowing and lending and pooling risks. Classes of these intermediaries include: deposit institutions .e.g. banks, insurance companies, trust companies .e.g. money managers, credit union and Mutual Funds. The financial systems within the financial institutions include: People (Investors and Borrowers), Place (Markets), Product (Securities .e.g. Treasury Bills), Price (Cost of Capital and Cost of Borrowing or simply interest.

Cost of Funds

When you get a loan from a bank, the bank charges interest on the loan. The interest that you get is the cost of lending the money. In other words, the bank could put the money to other use and earn a profit equivalent to or more than the interest that you pay on the loan. Cost of funds or the minimum required return a company should make on its own investments, to earn the cash flows out of which investors can be paid their

Cost of funds has three elements. First, the risk free-rate – this is the return one would get if a security was completely free of any risk. Second, risk free yields are typically on government securities, for example yields on Treasury Bills and third, the premium for business risk – this is an increase in the required rate of return due to compensate for existence of uncertainty about the future of a business.

Cost of funds can be cost of equity or cost of debt. Cost of equity could be estimated by dividend valuation model, which is based on the fundamental analysis theory. This theory states that the market value of shares is directly related to expected future dividends on the shares. The cost of debt capital already issued is the rate of interest (the internal rate of return), which equates the current market price with the discounted future cash receipts from the security.

Weighted Average Cost of Capital

In most cases, a company's funds may be viewed as a pool of resource, that is, a combination of different funds with different costs. Under such circumstances it might seem appropriate to use an average cost of capital for investment approval. High level of debt creates financial risk. Financial risk is measured by gearing ratio.

$$\frac{D}{E + D}$$

Higher gearing will increase KE (cost of equity)Where D stands for Debt and E stands for equity. As the level of gearing increase the cost of debt remain unchanged up to the certain level of gearing. The Ke (cost of equity) rises as the level of gearing increases (need for higher returns). The WACC does not remain constant but rather falls initially as proportional of debt increases and then begins to increase as the rising cost of equi ty/debt becomes more significant. The optimum level of gearing is where the company's weighted cost of capital is minimized. This assumes that WACC is unchanged coz of the following two factors: Cost of debt remains unchanged on the level of gearing increases. Cost of equity rises in such a way as to keep the WACC constant.

Managing People

Managing people is critical to the viability of any business. This is a call to learn and acquisition skills and competencies of managing employees or human resource. Many commentators say that the human resource is perceived as the best source competitive advantage. As pointed out earlier managing people deals with the productive use of people while satisfying the individual employee needs. This means that an entrepreneur has two goals to achieve. First, is to achieve organizational or business goals. These could be profit maximization or continuity of profits, business growth, increasing cash flow as well as increasing the market share. Second, is to satisfy the individual employees goals which include maximizing pay offs among others.

The art of managing people involves managing the flow of people into the organization. This deals with human resource functions such as recruitment and selection. Recruitment of staff also involve contractual relationships, in this case between employer or entrepreneur and employee. The term also includes redundancy, unfair dismissal and health and safety at work.

As stated earlier a contractual agreement with an employee must be enforceable as a contract may be oral or in writing. This is because there is generally no legal requirements that an agreement should be in writing for it to be treated by law as a legally binding contract. As a result an agreement will be enforced by law as a contract even though it is not in writing at all. In fact the largest number of contracts are never in writing.

After recruitment and selection comes managing the employees within the business. Successful entrepreneurs are required to understand performance management activities, the importance of training and development, the importance of considering rewarding staff. Additionally, there is also need to pay attention to the flowing out of employees. This involves managing employees exit from the organization.

Based on my personal observation and experience I have noted that employees in the employment setting they leave the organization in the following ways: first, is when an employee resign; second, is when an employee retires and lastly when an employee dies. In all these three areas an entrepreneur should be able to have skills of managing the existing employee.

Chapter 16

Create a Winning Recipe

After some trial and error in your business, you will figure out what works best. Once that happens, you will want to do the same thing over and over again. This is your recipe for success. *Just like a food recipe, a business recipe can be followed time and again to achieve the same result.* In fact, some believe that that is why money is called dough; you make your dough by using a recipe. In your business, your business dough recipe could be:

1. An ad that works 2.
2. A monthly mailer 3.
3. A sale that brings in customers
4. A monthly seminar
5. A stall at the Saturday public market
6. A billboard
7. Great locations
8. Almost anything that works and can be duplicated

If you think about it, repeating a successful formula is the hallmark of any well-run business. Budweiser sponsors sporting events because it knows that it will sell more beer if it does. Sponsoring sporting events is a tried and true business recipe. It works time and time again. Microsoft too has a recipe. We might call it "tweak and put out a new edition of Windows every few years." Microsoft knows that if it does so, it will be able to predictably count on those sales. Hollywood does the same thing.

Whereas no one knows for sure what movie people will like, Hollywood knows that it reduces the risk of failure if, for example, Tom Cruise or Julia Roberts stars in it. Getting a big name to star in a movie is a business recipe. If your business is going to be a long-term success, you will need to do the same thing. What will your recipe be? You need to experiment and figure out what works best.

After you do, long-term success will be much more likely if you reduce that thing, whatever it is, to a formula that you can repeat over and over again. In his great book, The E-Myth: Why Most Small Businesses Don't Work and What to Do About It, author Michael Gerber explains that many people go into business because they love something and want to make a living at it, a baker who loves to bake, for example.

Gerber makes it clear that what trips up the baker is that, while what he wants is to bake, being a business owner CREATE MULTIPLE PROFIT CENTERS. The problem for most small businesses is that they learn one good recipe, stick with it, run it into the ground, and never bother to figure out another one. The owner has learned only one method of making a buck. The problem with having just a single moneymaking formula is that it will inevitably be hit when the dreaded business cycle turns south. Just like the economy, all businesses have a business cycle.

The ice cream store sees sales spike in the summer and drop in the winter. Starbucks sees sales rise in the winter and drop in the summer. While experience will teach you, often the hard way, what your business cycle is, you can learn it much easier by speaking with people in your own line of work who have been around for a while. Once you know what your business cycle is, either through research or the school of hard knocks, you will want to minimize its effects on your business. One of the best ways to do that is to create multiple profit centers, a term coined by Barbara Winter in her book, Making a Living Without a Job.

The theory is essentially this: To succeed long-term in business, you need several recipes. You need to diversify your income. A smart stock investor does just that. He knows not to buy just one stock. That stock may go up, but it may go down. Having more than one stock ensures that when one stock does go down, the likelihood of taking a big financial hit is remote. His income is diversified. Your business must diversify as well if you are going to last.

Seven Secrets of Great Entrepreneurs

While the idea of being an Entrepreneur may start with a flicker, it often grows very bright. Even so, the question remains: Why are some Entrepreneurs more successful than others? Usually, it is because they know some things other Entrepreneurs do not. Here are the seven secrets of the great Entrepreneurs.

1. Be Willing to Take a Big Risk

Entrepreneurship is, as we have discussed, a risk.

When you quit your job to start a new business, there is no guarantee it will succeed, let alone succeed wildly. Cookie stores were nonexistent when Debbie Fields opened her first one in 1977. Today, Mrs. Field's Cookies numbers more than 1,000 stores. ***You have to be willing to look like a fool to succeed.*** If you are going to succeed wildly in your own business (and that is the idea), you too will need to take a risk. An intelligent, calculated gamble has the chance to hit big. Of course, it can also backfire, but that's why we play the game.

2. Dream Big Dreams

In the early 1950s, a young engineer named Douglas Englebart decided that rather than work for 51/2 million minutes for someone else (the amount of time that would elapse before he would turn 65), he would rather use his career to benefit man. He wanted to help people solve problems; that was the need he thought he could fill.

3. Value the Customer above all else

For Richard Branson, founder of the Virgin Group, the customer is king. For instance, he believed that many record stores suffered because the shoppingexperience was boring and the staff needed to enjoy their jobs more. Voilà! Virgin Megastore was born-a place stocked to the brim that has a great vibe where you can usually listen to the music you want before you buy it. It might help to know too that Branson started out not much different than the rest of us. His first business was a record store above a shoe shop in London, and he bartered for his rent

4. Take Care of Your People

This includes your employees, your investors, and your stockholders.

In 1913, Henry Ford said, "The wages we pay are too small in comparison with our profits. I think we should raise our minimum pay rate." Moreover, eight years later Ford introduced the first five-day work week, stating, "Every man needs more than one day for rest and recreation." And if ever there was an Entrepreneur who knew how to succeed, it was Ford.

5. Persevere

As I said, entrepreneurship is a risk and, as such, Entrepreneurs often fail. Many successful Entrepreneurs go bankrupt before they hit it big, but they stick with it anyway. In 1975, Microsoft's revenues were $16,000 and it had three employees. In 1976, revenues were $22,000 with seven employees. In both years, the company posted losses. Many companies would have quit after two such years, but most companies are not Microsoft.

6. Believe in Yourself

Buckminster Fuller, inventor of the geodesic dome and countless other tools, was an unknown, unhappy man when he decided to kill himself in 1927. But before he went through with it, he realized his problem had always been that he listened to others instead of himself. Then and there, he decided to trust his own intuition. Before he died, Fuller had revolutionized such disparate fields as architecture, mathematics, housing, and automobiles.

7. Have a Passion

A trait common to all great entrepreneurs is that they are passionate about what they do. Legendary investor and Entrepreneur, ***Charles Schwab*** *put it this way, "The person who does not work for the love of work but only for money is not likely to make money nor to find much fun in life."* Similarly, Anita Roddick, founder and managing director of Body Shop International, once said, "I want to work for a company that contributes to and is part of the community. I want something not just to invest in, I want something to believe in." In the end, maybe writer Joseph Campbell said it best, "If you follow your bliss, doors will open for you that wouldn't have opened for anyone else." That is the job before you—to find that bliss and turn it into profit. A challenge? Yes. But what a great challenge it is. The good news is that you need not be a world-famousEntrepreneur to think and act like one, and you need not reinvent the wheel either.

CHAPTER 17

Business on Shoestring

Bootstrap Financing

You may want to start a business but do not have enough money to do so. Are you out of luck? Nope. Actually, it is safe to say that most businesses start with less than optimum funding. According to the Small Business Administration (SBA), 60 percent of all new businesses begin as undercapitalized startups. So, you are in good company. But what it will take is hard work, pluck, and a tad of luck. Creating a shoestring business begins with finding the necessary funding (discussed in this chapter).

Ten Rules for bootstrapping a business

If you are going to bootstrap a business, there are some rules of the road you should know. As you go about getting the money you need to get started, it will help enormously to keep these ten tips in mind.

Rule 1:

You donot need a fortune to get started. It would be great if you had enough money, but just because you donot, it doesnot mean that you cannot start a business.

Rule 2:

Not all debt is bad debt. This is an adjunct to Rule 1. If you donot have enough money, then it is possible that you may have to incur debt to get going. But not all debt is bad debt. Some debt is good debt when it enables you to get ahead in life—to start a business, buy a home, finance college, etc. Most millionaires start out deeply in debt to finance their dream. Is it ideal? Of course not. But if you can take on some debt and see a way to pay it back through your business, it is not a bad option.

Rule 3:

Be frugal as an employee, you can waste supplies, make long distance calls, use FedEx, make too many copies, and spend your management budget without a second thought. But as a businessperson on a budget, you will have to learn to be lean and mean.

Rule 4:

Invest only in your best ideas. Remember that no business survives unless it is serving a market need. You may have many ideas, but faced with less money than ideal, you cannot afford to make mistakes. You must invest your time, money, and energy in only your best, most profitable ideas.

Rule 5:

Do what it takes. If you only are going to have 25 percent of the money that you need to start, then you must be willing to put in the other 75 percent in the form of time and effort. You will have to work harder and smarter than your competitors. You have to be willing to go the extra mile as a boot strapper.

Rule 6:

Look big. You may be starting a business out of your garage with no funds, but no one needs to know that. It is critical to your success that you project the image of a big, professional business. Until the business does get big and have some money, remember these two important words: Fake it! Beware of the Credit Card Trap While you can take out cash advances from your credit cards to start your business, be careful.

The credit card trap is easy to fall into but very hard to get out of. You know the trap, don't you? It follows this pattern: You charge for things you otherwise cannot afford or take out cash you have no way of paying back;

You run up balances on cards that charge you 18 percent interest(and up!); You pay only the minimum due each month, covering only the interest and service charge each month; You get stuck with a debt that never seems to go down.

Here is how to get out of the trap:

- After you have run up your cards, transfer all balances to the card with the lowest interest rate. This can save you a lot of money every month.
- Better yet, apply for a new card with a really low introductory "teaser" rate (e.g., 4.9%) and transfer all of your balances to that card.
- Once the teaser rate is set to expire, call that company and tell them that you will cancel the card unless they extend the rate for another six months. If they donot agree to do so, cancel the card, apply for another new card with a great rate, and transfer the balance again. This balance transfer dance can save you a ton of money.
- Pay off the total balance as soon as possible and always pay more than the minimum.

Rule 7:

Be creative. No money to hire that great Web designer? You better buy a book and learn a Web design program. Another option: barter. Another option: hire a student. As a boot strapper, you have to constantly be on guard for new ideas and new ways to bring in a buck.

Rule 8:

You got to believe! Northwestern University conducted a study of successful shoestring Entrepreneurs and discovered that they typically never owned a business before, had no business education, and, of course, didnot have enough money to start but did anyway. In short, they didnot know enough to be afraid.

Rule 9:

Have a passion. Wayne Huzienga started very small and eventually created Blockbuster Video, among many other businesses. Says Huzienga, "I don't think we are unique, we're certainly not smarter than the next guy. So, the only thing I can think of that I might do a little differently than some people isI work harder and when I focus in on something,I am consumed by it. It becomes a passion."

Rule 10:

Take care of your customers. You may not have as much money as the next guy. You may not have ads as big or a fleet of salesmen, but that does not mean you cannot be the best. One of the best ways to be the best is to offer personal, superior service to your customers.

Use of Other People's Money (OPM)

While it is difficult to start without enough money, it can be done. A far better solution when you donot have enough money to start a business is to get enough money using OPM—other people's money. Finding people who will be willing to invest in you will take determination; usuallyit isnot easy. Without collateral, perseverance will be essential.

Why? Because lenders and investors are skeptics, and they should be. Too many startups fail, so, accordingly, investors would rather put their capital into successful businesses that want to expand or startups that have already been partially funded. The unfunded startup is the riskiest investment of all. But it is also, potentially, the most lucrative, and you can use that fact to your advantage. If you are willing to share your pie, have a plan that makes economic sense, and are willing to look long and hard, the right investor can be found.

It is the possibility of a big return on their investment, coupled with the ability to write off a loss on their taxes, that makes the rich investor a viable alternative for the cash-strapped entrepreneur. The key will be your ability to entice the right person with the right deal. Investors want a high return. Ask them what they want, and give them what they want.

Most investors will want to know what you are putting into the venture, aside from your sweat equity. Be honest. If you are donating equipment or material, say so. If you are tapping credit cards, fess up. Your commitment can only help your cause. The key to winning over an investor or other lender is to look like a pro. Talking big without back-up facts will make you look a fool. Instead, come in looking like a businessman who understands business. You need facts, data, and hard figures that back up your rosy rhetoric.

You must know:

- How much you really need
- Why you need that much
- How much you can afford to pay back every month
- How you will make that amount

If you can answer these questions confidently, then it is time to go over your options because there are many ways to finance your business using OPM.

CHAPTER 18

Never Give Up But Work Hard, Hard, Hard

God's ordained assignment is not for the idle. Diligence simply means hard work. This means that whatever God has called you to do, pursue it diligently. You need to go about your vision with all diligence. Progress in life is a function of hard work. There is no food for a lazy man anywhere in this world. *Seest thou a man diligent in his business; he shall stand before kings; he shall not stand before mean men* (**Proverbs 22:29**).

Lazy and idle people never make headway in life, because they are not operating God's formula for successful living. For such people failure, disappointment and frustration are their portion. Victory and success will not find you in the house. You have to go out and search for it. *"Blessed shalt thou be when thou comest in and blessed shalt thou be when thou goest out"* (**Deuteronomy 28:6**)

This is a call not to sit down in your home and watch Televisionall day. You will fail to bring food on the table. Even if you pray, fast and speak in tongues, food will not come. Scriptures give Isaac in the book of Genesis. He was a hard worker in the land of the Philistines. He did not say that because it was God who sent me here then I don't have to work. The bible says that Isaac sowed in the land and in the same year he reaped a hundred-fold. ...Received in the same year a hundred-fold: and the Lord blessed him... *And the man waxed great, and went forward, and grew until he became very great (Gen 26:12-13).* It is God who prospers those that work hard. From the aforementioned scripture God prospered Isaac. He will prosper you too in your hard work and not in your laziness. And if a man also strive for masteries yet is he not crowned except he strive lawfully.

Timothy 2:15 says laziness is a destroyer and it puts man to a state of lack and begging. The more you engage yourself in diligence the better you become. It is more difficult to be located at the top without being diligent. I know many people that have not made it in life because of laziness.

There are many that run the race but it is only one that receives the price. He becometh poor that dealeth with a slack hand: but the hand of the diligent maketh rich"(Proverbs 10:4). Everyone that receives the prize in a competition does so after hard work. So, you need to press on and be diligent. It goes without saying that if you will not run and you do not work either from your own business or employment you will not eat.

The basis of an increase is output. If you are not a worker today be assured that tomorrow you will be a beggar and borrower that fails to pay back. *The wicked borrows and does not pay back but the righteous is gracious and gives"(Psalm 37:21).* If this happens to you and then you are dragged into a situation where you fail to bring food on the table, going without eating and reduced to a beggar, what a shame.

For even we were with you, this we commanded you, that if any would not work, neither should he eat (Thessalonians 3:10). God says the labour is worthy of his hirer (Luke 10:7). He is worth of his wages. So, what do you do to receive wages? Just labour. From this day, do not go home or go to bed with un accomplished list of items on your daily list. Life does not give you what you deserve, that is why you must fight for it.

Organization

Arrange your office for maximum performance and efficiency. Plenty of natural light where possible, adequate desk space, comfortable chair, and everything you need to perform any possible work-related task. Put everything back where it belongs. At the end of the day, clear off your desk and return every file and document to its proper place. This way everything will be exactly where it should be when you need it the next time.

Insist on the essentials before you begin a project. Prior to starting, gather all the materials you need beforehand. For a writer, that may mean a complete package of research materials. For a builder, it may mean gathering all the tools and supplies needed. Collect what you need first so you can work until completion, without the need for an unnecessary break in productivity.

Avoid the temptation to stack paper on your desk. File it so you know exactly where it is. Minimize the number of times you handle each piece of paper. Capitalize on all the valuable resources that are right in front of you. Your own personal Rolodex of important contacts you can count on, can spare you a lot of needless searching. A good librarian can help you find information on anything and most are happy to do so. Government offices, the Internet as well as directories like the Yellow Pages canbe valuable sources of timesaving information. Use them.

Getting A Head Start

Create tomorrow's to-do list, today. Most of us are less productive towards the end of the day. Assuming that the day's critical tasks have been completed, it is time to prepare for the next day. It is best to keep your to-do lists in your day planner or in a bound journal. This way you will have a permanent record of all your daily events and activities.

Start off with a clean desk every morning. Get rid of any backlog of work before you leave at night. If you can get in the habit of clearing your desk as you wind down the workday, you will have conquered a big obstacle to clear and creative thinking—clutter. You simply cannot perform at your best when faced with a mountain of paperwork, and a full load of tasks that must be done at the same time.

Do the worst thing first.

When faced with a list of unpleasant duties, tackle the most repulsive one first. After that, everything else is a breeze! You will feel unbeatable for the rest of the day. Get started immediately. Take the "Just Do It" approach. If you donot start,you will never finish. If you wait for conditions to be just right, you may miss out altogether. ***Do something every day that will move you closer to your goals.***

Donot put it off. Do it now

Be punctual. Develop punctuality into a habit. Immediately you will gain an advantage over 97% of the population. Consistently being on time makes you look good and saves time and money. It also indicates respect for others' time. Arriving early gives you extra time to get acquainted with new people and facilities… time to relax… time to mentally prepare… or simply time to review your notes.

Give yourself the advantage of an early start in the morning. Get up one hour earlier than normal and put that hour to good, productive use. Try it for a month and you may be astonished at what this one little hour can do for you. It is an easy way to gain a distinct advantage. Begin each individual task on a positive note. Get something important done at the very beginning and you will feel a sense of accomplishment thatcan carry you through the day. With simple projects, maybe it is the first oneon the list. For the more complex, perhaps it is preparing a detailed action plan. Keep this simple idea in mind with every task or project and you will getoff to a great start every time.Peak Productivity Ideas

Work on the single, most important task at any given time. The most important task is the one that gives you the greatest value or the highest possible return. Constantly ask yourself, "What is the most valuable use of my time, right now?" Then, do the most productive thing possible.

Stick with it!

Continue to stay focused on that one priority item, regardless. Work at it relentlessly. Take it as far as you can go without breaking your concentration, no matter how difficult, unpleasant, or challenging the situation may be. This often requires a strong will on your part, but the payoff is worth it.

Go to the next, most important item on your list. Focus your attention 100% on this task until it is completed. When you are done, or you have taken it as far as you possibly can, revert to the next item in succession on your list. One by one, you will finish each task, always working on the most important one.

Do only that to which you bring unique value. Delegate or purchase the rest. This is a form of leverage and it can be very effective. Do the key tasks— those that you're best at-- yourself. Whatever skill, experience and expertise you bring to the table should be used effectively, as the situation warrants it. Utilize your time and your expertise wisely. Look at each task and determine the most effective use of available resources.

Transform downtime into productive activity

Determine your time of peak productivity and do your most intense, demanding work then. Use other, less productive times to return calls, send faxes, hold meetings and carry on discussions. No one can be at their peak at all times of the day. The secret is to know when you are most effective and to use that time for the most important and demanding work.

Use your computer efficiently

Get in the habit of writing things once and then editing wherever necessary on screen. Avoid preparing hand-written notes that later need to be entered into your computer. Learn to use data-bases, project planners, spreadsheets, or whatever programs fit your business and your role in it.

Economize your time

Accomplish tasks with less waste. The fewer steps involved to complete a task, the better. Work at improving efficiency by shaving minutes or even seconds off routine duties. Be on the lookout for overlap, excessive handling, unnecessary steps and duplication of work.

Mix-up the size of tasks to avoid burnout. Instead of taking on two 4-hour projects, one after another, break them apart with a 30-minute task in between. Strive for a blend of tasks from small to large. You will feel a stronger sense of accomplishment and be less drained at the end of the day.

Challenge yourself to finish jobs ahead of schedule. Constantly seek out better, faster, more productive ways of doing things. Give yourself a reward for your increased productivity. Strive for incremental improvements. Small but consistent improvement in effort and results can make a dramatic difference over the long haul. All you need is to do things just slightly better than average with regularity and you will be in the top 5% of all achievers.

Develop a preference for action

Never put off until tomorrow, what you can do today. Dig in without delay and you will accomplish far more in ten years than the vast majority will accomplish in a lifetime. Do it now and you will feel a wonderful sense of accomplishment. How you use your time determines the quality of life you create.

Decide what you want to accomplish more than anything else. What one item on your list, or what goal is most important to you at this very moment. That is the one thing you need to focus on. Follow this path first above all others. You can achieve whatever you really want but... you can only accomplish one thing at a time.Build upon each accomplishment by moving right along to the next task at hand.

As you achieve one thing after another, you increase your potential for higher achievement. Success begets success. Each task completed successfully, fuels your momentum and builds up your confidence to achieve more. Every successful accomplishment strengthens your foundation to meet the next challenge. Do one thing at a time and then quickly move on. Turn essential daily activities into powerful habits. A habit is something you just do automatically, without conscious deliberation. We all have tasks that are unpleasant or distasteful, yet necessary. Once it becomes a habit, it is much easier to endure. You donot have to stop and think about it.

Change old wasteful habits into productive ones

Decide to be a more effective time manager, starting today. Others will notice your ability to get things done, regardless. You will be appreciated more and you will have more time to take advantage of the things you really enjoy.

Imagine you only have half a day to complete a full day of work. What would you do? What must be done first? What can be delegated to others or putoff until later? When you have suddenly got less time to work with, you are forced into a higher level of efficiency planning. Tactics, Techniques and Action Steps.

Eliminate personal interruptions

When you are on a roll, the last thing you want is to be stopped in your tracks by unnecessary intrusions. Great accomplishments occur when you gather momentum and a sense of rhythm as you progress towards a successful conclusion. Interruptions can hinder your success. Donot let it happen. Use controls such as door signs and voice mail. If you must, seek out a work space where no one else can find you. Or, adjust your hours to give you creative time at non-peak periods.

Learn to say no to low pay-off tasks. It is easy to be busy with less important work. If the task is not important today, donot waste your time on it. The fewer low pay-off items you work on, the more productive you will be. Wipe out any unnecessary travel. Take advantage of today's time-saving technology. Wherever possible, use the telephone, fax machine or e-mail to deal with the important issues of the day. Avoiding personal visits frees up time for more productive work.

Speak your thoughts into a cassette recorder, or use voice-recognition software and then edit your spoken words into the appropriate format. This is an easy way to express your ideas, without trying to "write" the perfect piece. For many people, writing is a chore—but talking is easy, as long as it is not to an audience. In many cases, the most effective writing is a one-on-one personal communication.

Introduce daily deadlines

Like them or not, deadlines increase productivity. The closer we get to an impending deadline, the more we are pressured into doing whatever it takes to complete the task. Institute a series of deadlines—monthly... weekly... daily. As each deadline approaches, the real work begins. Deadlines can give your productivity a significant boost as long as you stick to them.

Stand up while communicating on the telephone

Standing helps you get right to the point, for a faster, more productive call. It is easy to get a little too comfortable while sitting and phone conversations seem to drag on longer. Return all telephone calls at one point in the day, preferably after you have completed your crucial action to-do list. Completing several small tasks at once is easier as you build the momentum. Consolidating your efforts helps you make the most of your time.

Cluster together small jobs like banking and post office pick-up/delivery, or data-base updating and responding to e-mail messages. When you are forced to shift from one type of activity to another and back again, you lose time trying to re-focus and re-gain momentum. Conduct meetings efficiently.

Challenge yourself

Always try to beat your personal best. Focus your attention on finding a better, more efficient way of doing the same task before you. By making it a game, you can turn even the most mundane task into something that is interesting and fun.

Start your to-do list on a single, full-size sheet of paper. List everything, without concern for where it might fit in sequence. After listing all tasks, identify the 3 specific groups of tasks (A's, B's &C's) by using different colored markers. Once prioritized, you can then re-organize them easily into your day planner in the right sequence. This way, as you start each day, all your critical tasks are already laid out for you.

Group all your important records together

Maintain only one to-do list and one day planner. Preferably, your to-do list should be a part of your planner. Keep permanent records and avoid making notes on envelopes and small shreds of paper. Use your planner/notebook for all documentation. To try and utilize more than one list is unproductive duplication. You also run the risk of missing a key element while transferring bits of data.

Get right to the point in all communications

Avoid the long and wasteful windup. ***Keep your message short and sweet wherever possible.*** Trim the fat and the filler. Be respectful of others time and they will return the favor. If you rely exclusively on your computer's hard drive to keep records, sooner or later you are bound to experience a frustrating crash that could wipe out everything. Computers can and do fail.

If that is all you have, without back-up, you could face serious frustrations. Build a paper trail, so you always have back-up to prevent any possible mishap. Catch yourself achieving and reward yourself with glowing praise. Life, in many respects, is a mind game. Sometimes playing little tricks and games with ourselves can stimulate new levels of productivity and accomplishment. A little positive self-talk for goals reached can help you achieve more.

Add incentives to trigger greater effort. Promise yourself or your team, something that would really be enjoyed, if you can reach your target on time. Dangle a big enough carrot and you will find creative ways to overcome obstacles and achieve goals in record time.Post your plan. Keeping a visible record of your progress as you work away at a difficult project can spur you on to greater achievements. Use your outline as a checklist and mark off each individual task as it is completed. This helps you to stay on track, maintain motivation and provides visual proof of accomplishment.

Start somewhere other than the beginning. Sometimes it is best to just get started at any point on a project. Trying to stick to the start-to-finish protocol you learned in school, may be counter-productive. If the beginning is causing you difficulty, skip it and move on to something you can do right away. Take the easiest step, and do it first. Then go on to the next easiest.

Take some form of productive action immediately

Know that your moment of power is NOW. Nothing in the past… and nothing in the future is as vital as the moment before you right now. The only time you can count on with certainty are those moments that lie before you today. Do not waste them.

Produce forms to reduce duplication of creative energies. Prepare generic documents that can be used for similar applications, over and over again. Fax cover sheets, meeting agenda forms, questionnaires, and testimonial requests are but a few examples of documents that can be standardized for widespread use.

Act as your own coach

On days when you are tempted to wander from the most important task, catch yourself and adjust your course. The easiest way to develop self-motivation is to keep your main goal in view at all times. The goal is the reasonwhy you are doing what you are doing. Having a goal in mind, something that you are working toward, gives you the fuel you need to get through the tough times.

Face challenges and difficulties head-on. Often the most important task at any given time is the least appealing. When that is the case, the best thing to do is to roll up your sleeves and get to work. Dig in. Usually it is not as bad as you have imagined. Delegate wherever possible. Follow-up to make sure others are on track and on time. Often, individual tasks can be handled by others. Utilizing the resources of others can be a big help where adequate direction and training has been provided.

Establish an efficient filing system.

Nothing is more frustrating than knowing you have the materials you need… and not being able to locate them. One way of adding efficiency to filing is to create an index page and place it at the front of each file drawer. Categories can be numbered systems or alphabetical listings, as long as there is plenty of room for relevant additions. As you add a new file to the draw, note it on the index. Put everything in its rightful place and it will be there when you need it.

Keep your day planner (preferred) or a notebook within reach at all times.

Record all your ideas, thoughts, concepts and any other information that can pop into your mind at anytime… and often does while you are busy doing other things. Make note of non-urgent issues you wish to share with others and do so at the end of the workday.

Make decisions quickly and firmly. People who get things done in life seem to share the characteristic of making quick decisions and sticking with them. Donot waste time deliberating. Size up the situation as best you can and decide. Not all decisions can be made that quickly, but day-to-day type of decisions can be. The more you practice this, the better and more efficient you will become.

PART III

STARTING AND GROWING A GREAT SUCCESSFUL BUSINESS

CHAPTER 19

Creativity, Invention and Innovation

After allI read on the blogs and Twitter, and all the new innovation programmes and initiatives in state and local governments. I feel the need to revisit the definitions of these key words: innovation, creativity and inventions.

First the innovation definitions

As indicated earlier an Entrepreneur is a person who starts a new business. That is not necessarily innovative, but it can create new jobs and new wealth, so it is valuable. Sometimes Entrepreneurs create new wealth, so it is valuable. Sometimes, Entrepreneurs create businesses based on new ideas, either through inventions or new inventions. However, a person running a McDonald's is also an Entrepreneur, but not necessarily innovative.

What is Creativity?

Creativity simply means creating value and it is directly linked with invention and it is turned into practical reality through innovation. Entrepreneurship then sets that innovation in the context of an enterprise which is something of recognized value.

Creativity is the act of turning new and imaginative ideas into reality. Creativity is characterized by the ability to perceive the world in new ways, to find hidden patterns, to make connections between seemingly unrelated phenomena, and to generate solutions. *Creativity involves two processes: thinking, then producing. If you have ideas, but donot act on them, you are imaginative but not creative.*

"Creativity is the process of bringing something new into being.

Creativity requires passion and commitment. It brings to our awareness what was previously hidden and points to new life. The experience is one of heightened consciousness: ecstasy." – Rollo May, The Courage to Create *is* this possible in business? I believe so, but you have to be willing to take risks and progress through discomfort to get to the finish line.

"A product is creative when it is (a) novel and (b) appropriate. A novel product is original not predictable. The bigger the concept, and the more the product stimulates further work and ideas, themore the product is creative."

—Sternberg &Lubart, *Defying the Crowd*

What is Innovation?

*Innovation is the implementation of a new or significantly improved product, service or process that creates value for business, government or society.*Some people say creativity has nothing to do with innovation— that innovation is a discipline, implying that creativity is not. Well, I disagree. Creativity is also a discipline, and a crucial part of the innovation equation. There *is* no innovation without creativity. The key metric in both creativity and innovation is value creation.

An inventor is someone who creates a new to the world product or solution. Inventions become interesting when they create value for the inventor or consumers or the world at large. Inventors are innovative, but innovative solutions donot have to be inventions. Many innovations are new business models, new services experience that are not necessarily "innovations."

Just as Entrepreneurs are not defined simply as owner – managers, entrepreneurial firms are not defined, necessarily, in terms of size. But there are linkages between size and innovation. Few small firms introduce really new products into their product mix. Even fewer introduce really new products into the economy as a whole. This role is likely to be taken by larger firms because of the resources they command. However, small firms can and often do introduce products or services that are clearly differentiated from those of the competition. Indeed, this ability to differentiate clearly is a major element in the success. Is this innovation?

Perhaps it is, but one would have to stretch Schumpeter's first or even his third criterion (opening new market to accommodate it).

Innovation is the process of translating an idea or invention into a good or service that createsvalue or for which customers will pay. To be called an innovation, an idea must be replicable at an economicalcost and must satisfy a specific need. Innovation involves deliberate application of information, imagination and initiative in deriving greater or different values from resources, and includes all processes by which new ideas are generated and converted into useful products. In business, innovation often results when ideas are applied by the company in order to further satisfy the needs and expectations of the customers. In a social context, innovation helps create new methods for alliance creation, joint venturing, flexible work hours, and creation of buyers' purchasing power.

Innovations are divided into two broad categories:

1. *Evolutionary innovations* (continuous or dynamic evolutionary innovation) that are brought about by many incremental advances in technology or processes and
2. *Revolutionary innovations* (also called discontinuous innovations) which are often disruptive and new.

Innovation is synonymous with risk-taking and organizations that create revolutionary products or technologies take on the greatest risk because they create new markets. Imitators take less risk because they will start with an innovator's product and take a more effective approach. Examples are IBM with its PC against AppleComputer, Compaq with its cheaper PC's against IBM, and Dell with its still-cheaper clones against Compaq.

Use innovation in a sentence

By allowing the developer of an innovation to reap the rewards of his efforts, we create an environment that encourages innovative thinking and hard work.Sofia was much happier at this workplace: they celebrated innovation and rewarded employees who came up with new ideas and better ways of doing things. Some people praise technology and innovation but I think we should go back to the dark ages because as a society we would be much happier.

Therefore, an innovation can also be defined as a new idea that is put into a valuable or profitable action. An innovation can be created by an inventor who then licenses his or her invention to others to commercialize the concept in his or her capacity as an Entrepreneur. An innovation can be created by the organization to disrupt an existing market. Innovation can happen in organization of any size. Additionally, there is innovation in governments, in academic institutions and in not – for profits. We typically donot think of these organizations as entrepreneurial or as inventing new things yet they can be innovative. Further, innovations can be new products, but can also be new service models, new business models and new customer experiences.

The ability to sport opportunities and to innovate are the most important distinguished features of Entrepreneurs. Innovation is the prime tool Entrepreneurs use to create or exploit opportunity. These characteristics set Entrepreneurs apart from owner – managers. Entrepreneurs link innovation to the market place so as to exploit an opportunity and make their business grow.

We need all the three of these concepts work well to succeed. We need inventors to create new products and new processes and we need Entrepreneurs to disrupt existing markets and bring these new products and services to the market. We also need innovation from large existing firms, because without innovation they stagnate and die. When we talk about innovation, invention and Entrepreneurs and when we put policies in place to encourage certain types of activities or investments we need to understand the implications and ramifications of those words and actions. While closely related, invention, innovation and Entrepreneurs are not the same things and should not be treated in the same fashion.

There is a fundamental difference between an innovator and an inventor, writes digital Entrepreneur Tom Grasty in a great column over at MediaShift Idea Lab.

Invention is the "creation of a product or introduction of a process for the first time." Thomas Edison was an inventor.

Innovationhappens when someone "improves on or makes a significant contribution" to something that has already been invented.

Okay, so they are different. What does that mean for Entrepreneurs?

You cannot just focus on innovation and you cannot just focus on invention. That is not what an Entrepreneur does. The Entrepreneur recognizes the potential early on, then turns it into something big.

Grasty explains it with an analogy:"If invention is a pebble tossed in the pond, innovation is the rippling effect that pebble causes. Someone has to toss the pebble. That is the inventor. Someone has to recognize the ripple to eventually become a wave. That is the Entrepreneur.

"Entrepreneurs don not stop at the water's edge. They watch the ripples and spot the next big wave *before* it happens. And it is the act of anticipating and riding that "next big wave" that drives the innovative nature in every entrepreneur."

CHAPTER 20

Getting Started

Preparation in Getting the Basics Right for Starting a Great Successful Business is at the heart and souls of entrepreneurship."People become successful the minute they decide to." In respect to preparation in Ecclesiastes 3, we are told that there is a time for everything. You have to ask God "When" for your assignment. God knows the perfect time for you to set out.

Moses in the book of Exodus struck for 40 years earlier than God's time. This sent him on personal exile, he was downgraded. Jesus, the son of God, was the natural son of Joseph for 30 years, until He became manifested in His assignment. ***For which of you intending to build a tower sitteth not down first and counteth the cost whether he have sufficient to finish it (Luke 14:28). Lest haply after he hath laid the foundation and is not able to finish it all that behold it begin to mock him saying this man began to build and was not able to finish (Luke 14:29-30)***During the preparation time is when you need to set goals and proper planning in terms of required resources and setting priorities. There is what is called "the fullness of time".

It is the right time to step out into your God given assignment after a good preparation. You need to be sensitive to the right time, in order to make healthy progress. So, prepare before stepping out into your great business and you will succeed.

Conceiving Ambition

This is one's expectation or what one looks forward to achieving. Thus, it is a self – made plan. "Without vision the people perish." Ambition therefore has the potential to failure and can even destroy the ambitious one. Only the ambition that falls in line with God's drawn-out vision becomes fruitful and successful. Absalom was ambitious and his ambition killed him!

Dr. David Oyedepo says, "Ambition says, I want it by all means", but vision says, "I have it because God says it, and I am in His plan." Ambitions contrary to God's vison are cousins of anxiety, whereas vision is a relative of peace.

Talents Skills, competencies and abilities

Talents, skills, competencies and abilities are required for you to achieve your goal, impressions and ambitions of owning or running a successful great business. This is a call to clarify them and craft superior strategies to multiply and maximize them.

When clarifying them you need to develop absolute clarity about who you are, what you want and the best way to achieve it. This leads to multiplication of your talents, skills, competences and abilities from which you leverage yourself and other people's customers, knowledge, ability, efforts, money and resources. To achieve this comes the need to determine your special talents, skills, competencies, abilities and strengths and focus on developing them to a higher level.

Become a great leader

Starting or growing a successful great business requires you to become a great leader. Your personal leadership ability is the major limit on what you can achieve. Leadership is the major factor for business success. Leadership is the ability to get results through influence and this requires you to have a clear vision of the future of your great business and take courage to act even in the absence of guaranteed success.

Responsibilities of leadership include; setting and achieving business goals, market and innovate – continuously seek faster, better, cheaper, easier ways to create and keep customers, set priorities and work on key tasks while supervising results. Additionally, leadership also involves solving problems, making decisions, leading by example, performing and getting results.

Effective Management of Resources

To run a successful great business requires effective management of a variety of resources such as great people, equipment, property, cash, great brand, great product or service and inventory. Of all these resources, cash is probably the most important. With sufficient cash a business has the ability to buy any of the other resources in which it may be deficient.

Whether the purchase of that resource is worthwhile at the price required is another matter, but the purchase can still be made. All the resources other than cash have a value to a business that is dependent on their availability, utilization, market demand and prevailing economic climate. It is cash and only cash that maintains a constant value and can easily be turned into other assets or resources.

Confirmation

This is seeking the affirmation of others in deciding what steps to take in starting your great business. God is never moved by multitudes or by popular opinion. If all the prophets in the world prophesy you into a successful great business and yet God has not ordained it that way, that business will fail. *I have not sent these prophets yet they run. I Have not spoken to them yet they prophesy, (Jeremiah 23:21).*

Many people are running a race they have not been assigned to run and results are failure. If you go into businesses that God has not confirmed or ordained, be assured that you will finance that business yourself. So, stop being led by men, rather, be led by God. If you let God lead you, then you shall not want! No amount of confirmation by people can put words into His mouth.

What He has not said, He has not said; what He has not written, He has not written. Locate His writing about you, not writings of men. Human confirmation is, more often than not, confusion is disguise.

Choosing a Great Name

Now that you have a good idea about what your business is going to be and where you are headed with it, it is time to begin to put your foundation in place. You will need to structure the business legally, get the necessary licenses and permits, and get funding. But before you can do any of those things, it is time to have some fun. You need to name your business and, in all likelihood, find a location for it. Remember Location, Location, and Location.

What is in a Name? Naming your business should be enjoyable, but for some people, it is stressful. What if you pick the wrong name? What if the name you pick has already been taken? While it is smart to be cautious, it is nothing to get overly concerned about.The important thing to realize is that your business name will become your alter ego, so be sure to pick a name that reflects on you and your business well. How do you pick a name? You have three options. The first is to pick a name that says exactly what your business is. Begin with what your business is going to do and the image you want to express.

Include both in the actual name of the business or reflect those ideas in the name, so that when people hear your business name, they know what you are offering. Be sure the name is not already in local use and that it is not too similar to that of a competitor. Try to pick one that is catchy and memorable; alliteration often works well. Also, be sure to pick a name that is not difficult to pronounce or spell.

When people call directory assistance, you want them to be able to find you. After you come up with five names that you really like, get some feedback from people you trust; they may not think your name is as good as you think it is. Remember, your business has to serve a market need, so finding out what the market thinks about your proposed business name, even in a small and informal way, is smart. The second method of business-name creation is to pick a name that is totally unique and has nothing to do with your business at all.

Choose names that are great because they are so unique that they are memorable. The risk here is that while your name may be unique, it may be too odd and obscure for people to remember it. Trademark concerns while making your final decision regarding your name, it is important to do a trademark search to see if the name already has been trademarked. If it has, you may not be able to use it. Different names are given different degrees of trademark protection.

A trademark is a distinctive word, phrase, or logo that is used to identify a business. Nike and its unique swoosh symbol are protected under trademark law because they are distinctive. Other words are given far less protection. Common or ordinary words that are not inherently distinctive get much less, or no, trademark protection, even if someone tries to trademark them. Licenses, Permits, and Business Formation Deciding what legal form your business should take is not the most scintillating of topics, but it may be one of the most important decisions you will make.

The form your business takes can determine how big it may grow, who can invest in it, and who is responsible should it get in trouble. It is a critical decision. Once decided, it is then important to handle some other legal issues, namely getting the requisite licenses and permits required by your city, county, or state.

Business Formation

There are three forms your business can take. It can be a sole proprietorship, a partnership, or a corporation, and each of the last two have subsets. When deciding which of these is best for you, it would behoove you to speak with both your lawyer and your account, because each choice has different legal and financial considerations to weigh. Below is an overview that you can use as a launching pad for discussions with your own advisors.

Sole Proprietorships and General Partnerships

A sole proprietorship is the cheapest and easiest form of business you can start. Simply decide on a name for your business, get a business license, file and publish a fictitious business name statement, hang your shingle, and voilà! You are in business. The downside to sole proprietorship is significant: You and the business are legally the same thing.

If something goes wrong, say as a chiropractor you accidentally injure someone, not only is your business at risk, but so are your personal assets. Your home, cars, bank accounts, everything is at risk when you are a sole proprietor. Another problem with this form of business is that you have no partners to work with or bounce ideas off of.

It is a dangerous way to do business. Therefore, having a teammate is why operating a business as a partnership becomes attractive. Essentially, a business partnership is a lot like a marriage. You need to pick a good partner because you will be spending a lot of time together and trusting each other. And, as with a sole proprietorship, in a general partnership, both you and your partner are personally liable for the debts of the business.

The danger is that your partner can make some dumb decisions and get the partnership into debt, and you will be personally responsible for that debt. So, as you can see, while there are many good aspects to having a partner, partnerships are fraught with danger. You have to weigh the benefits against the burdens and decide if bringing in a partner is right for you.

Another thing to be wary of is the emotional aspect of having a partner. One advantage to being a sole proprietor, and thus the only boss, is you have no one to answer to except yourself. That is one of the definite perks of being a solo entrepreneur. Bringing in a partner means you will have to consider another point of view before any major decision is made. Also, when partnerships do not work out, best friends who become partners do not always stay best friends.

On the other side of the ledger, there are many things to be said for having a business partner. One is that, it enables you to have someone with whom to brainstorm. That great idea you have may not be such a great idea after all, and a partner you trust can tell you why. A partner also gives you another pair of hands to do the work. It is difficult to be the one who has to do everything when you are solo. Partners alleviate that.

Last, and certainly not least, having a business partner gives you someone to share the financial responsibilities of the business. That is not insignificant. Having considered the pros and cons, having concluded that a partner can help more than it might hurt, and maybe even knowing someone you would like to partner with, it is still a good idea that you "date" first before jumping in. Find a project or two and work together.

See how you get along, how your styles mesh (or donot), how you deal with deadlines, and whether the union enhances your work.

Remember, you will be spending a lot of time with your partner, so you need to be sure that you work well together, have a good time, and have skills that complement one another. Finally, get some work references and make some phone calls. Deciding to partner with someone is one of the most important decisions you can make in your small business, so donot skimp on the homework. As far as the costs go, the licensing and permits are fairly insignificant. The main cost is hiring a business lawyer to draft the partnership agreement.

Limited Partnerships

There are two classes of partnerships: general partnerships (discussed above) and limited partnerships. In a general partnership, all partners are equal. Each partner has equal power to incur obligations on behalf of the partnership, and each partner has unlimited liability for the debts of that partnership. Because not all partnerships require that the partners have equal power and liabilities, some partnerships decide to form as a limited partnership instead. In a limited partnership, there is usually only one general partner (although there could be more). The other partners are called limited partners, hence the name limited partnership. In a limited partnership, the general partner or partners have full management responsibility and control of the partnership business on a day-to-day basis.

The general partner runs the show and makes the decisions. A limited partner cannot incur obligations on behalf of the partnership and does not participate in the daily operations and management of the partnership. In fact, the participation of a limited partner in the partnership is usually nothing more than initially contributing capital and hopefully later receiving a proportionate share of the profits. A limited partner is essentially a passive investor.

While the general partner has all of the power, he or she also has the lion's share of the liability. A limited partner's liability is capped at the amount of his or her financial contribution to the partnership. Should the truck of a limited partnership kill someone accidentally, the damaged party could go after the general partner's personal, but would be limited to the limited partner's capital contribution. Thus, the main advantage to this business entity is that it allows the general partner the freedom to run the business without interference, and gives the limited partners diminished liability if things go wrong.

Although a limited partner may seek to be more involved in the day-to-day operations of the partnership, he or she does so at some risk. If he or she does participate more, it is altogether possible that he or she may be viewed as a general partner in the eyes of the law, with its attendant liability risks. Another key benefit of the limited partnership is that it pays no income tax. Income and losses are attributed proportionally to each partner and accounted for on their respective tax returns.

Because of this flow-through tax treatment, a limited partnership is often the structure of choice for real estate ventures and investment securities groups. If you do decide to start your business as a limited partnership, have your partnership agreement drafted by an attorney.

Incorporating

The best thing about forming your business as a corporation is that it limits your personal liability, which is not true for partnerships and sole proprietorships. For example, say that you owned a tire shop and one of your employees negligently installed a tire that fell off a car and caused a three-car accident with several personal injuries.

If your tire store was not a corporation, the injured parties could come after you personally for monetary damages. This means that you could lose your business, your house— everything. That would not be true if you incorporated. Creditors are limited to the assets of the corporation only for payment and may not collect directly from the shareholders. There are several types of corporations including limited liability companies, closely held corporations, professional corporations, and S and C corporations.

Outfitting the Office

The actual process of setting up your business will involve dealing with plenty of details—details that must be understood and organized before you open the doors; details that must be handled and forgotten so that you can go onto other, more important matters; details that can sink or swim your business.

Automating Your Office

Whatever your business, you must computerize it. Whether it involves tracking sales, writing letters, or inventory control, starting out with a good computer system is vital. Although it may seem less expensive to do certain office tasks by hand rather than investing in a good computer system or related software, that is fuzzy logic for two reasons.

First, you eventually will automate whatever tasks you begin by hand. Changing over later will take longer and cost more. Second, computer hardware and software will allow you to be more effective and, thus, more productive from the get-go. Computers represent a solid investment of your startup capital. Do not skimp in this area. Throughout this book you have been, and will be, cautioned to keep your overhead low. High overhead will eat up your profits and your precious cash flow quickly. But this is not one of those times.

The rapid pace of technological change means that computers usually become obsolete within three or four years. If you buy a used one, or an older or a slower model, you are simply speeding up the moment when you will have to buy a new one. Be smart and buy a good computer and the necessary software now. You have likely learned a thing or two about purchasing computers since you bought your first one. You are more knowledgeable about your computer needs, and you probably know what areas you would like to improve. It may be that your monitor is too small and you want a larger one, or that you want a newer operating system. Probably what you want is speed and more speed.

Creating a Great Image

At the height of the e-commerce boom, an executive from a well-established "old-economy" company was hired to be the new CEO of a young, brash, well-financed Internet start-up. For his first day at his new company, the CEO decided to look his best. He dressed in an expensive suit and his favorite tie. That day, he was to address the company's 100-plus employees. As he tells the story, he felt sharp, and looked great. The new CEO gave an enthusiastic, short introductory speech and then opened the floor to questions. The room was utterly and completely silent. Seconds seemed like hours as people refused to participate. "Come on," he implored, "ask me a question."

Finally, someone yelled out, "Why are you wearing a tie?" As in life, first impressions are awfully important in business too. After someone encounters you and your business for the first time, they will leave with an impression. It may be positive, it may be negative. They may think yours is a well-run, professional enterprise that will provide them with a great service, or not. One thing you can bank on though is that the first impression will very likely be the lens that they use to view your company forever.

Think about it in your own life. If you meet someone for the first time and he acts like a real jerk, don't you label him a jerk? It doesnot matter that he might have been having a bad day. He becomes "the jerk." When you go to a business for the first time and get bad service, don't you usually conclude that their business doesnot deserve your continued patronage? That is why they say that you only have one chance to make a great first impression.

The Importance of a Great Image Although image isnot everything, it is not insignificant. Your signs, business cards, letterhead, logo, and store/office say much about who you are. Combined, these things constitute your business identity. A professional business identity says that, even though you are new, you are to be taken seriously.

Of course, you will have to back up that great image with great products or services and customer service. But to get people to understand that yours is a business worth patronizing, you have to open the door by having a sharper image. That is the task before you.

Your Logo

A logo is one of the first things you need to create because it will be used on your letterhead, business cards, and other documents. It will distinguish your company, set a tone, and foster your desired image. You want a logo that exemplifies who you are and what it is you do.

When creating a logo, you have two options: you can do it yourself or hire someone to do it for you. If you decide to design your own logo, you will need a software program that offers graphics, clip art, and photographs that can be incorporated into your logo. It is important that you not use any material that is copyrighted in your logo design. If you can afford to hire someone to create a logo for you, do it.

Elements of your image

These items need to be coordinated and thematic in order to create a dynamic business identity and image:

Your Brochure

Not every business will need or use a brochure. Even if a brochure is not traditionally part of businesses like yours, it still might be a great way to create a professional image and bring in business. The thing to be wary of is spending money on a brochure if it really does nothing to add to your business. A brochure can be an expensive item and thus not worth the money if you really donot need it.When creating a brochure, avoid the following:

Making it too busy: Creating a brochure that is so jampacked with informationthat it is unpleasing to the eye and difficult to read is a sure way to waste money. It is much better to keep paragraphs short, use white space, use bullets, and keep it simple.

Making the cover boring: Too many businesses think that headlining their brochure with their business name is a sure way to entice people to read more.If you want people to read your brochure, you must catch their attention (usually with some benefit they could get by reading more) and draw them in. Ask yourself: What is the purpose of this brochure? Is it an introduction to your business, a selling tool, both, or more? Whatever your answer, your brochure needs to reflect the same values, tone, and theme that will be found in your other image-creating materials.

Use your logo. Use your colors. Reinforce your desired image with text and graphics that reflect your business image.

SIGNS:

A big, bold, visible sign in the right location(s) can be one of the best tools for creating an image, as well as generating new business. Signs are obviously most used for retail businesses, especially when drop-in traffic is a key element to your business model. Signs come in many forms, from cheap wood ones to expensive electrical and glass models. The same considerations that are used in your other materials apply here. If you can get the image of each of your materials to reinforce an overall theme, busy people who don't yet know of your business will easily understand what it is you are about if they are met with consistency. Choosing the right sign especially is an area where professional expertise is useful. How big should the sign be? What should it say? How big should the letters be? Creative and Design companies will help you figure this all out.

Your Website

Even if your business has nothing to do with the Internet, you cannot pass up the chance to create an online image. Indeed, a Website has become a business necessity. Not only is it an inexpensive way to buttress your image and tell people who you are, but it is also an opportunity to sell more, get more customers, make more money, and impress strangers. And you need not be Amazon.com to be successful. In fact, you probably don't want to be.

Your business Website should, in all likelihood, be a clean, simple, elegant place that does a few things very well. Your home page should explain what your business is and what the Web site is about. It should be simple and easy to load. Inside, your business addresses and contact information should be easy to find. Features and benefits of working with you should be prominent. Beyond that, what you do with your site is up to you. You may want to consider having some features that keep people coming back, because the more they come back to your site, the more likely it is they will buy from you.

You can offer such things as: INTERACTIVITY. E-commerce interactivity means providing interactive tools that enable potential customers to learn more about your products. It could also mean offering chat rooms, message boards, or newsletters. Streaming video is a possibility. MEMBERS ONLY AREAS. Some businesses offer members only domains on their Web sites, where they offer access to premium information, tools, and services. Think about AOL for a moment. It is nothing but a huge member only Web site; not a bad model.

CHAPTER 21

Develop a Successful Business Plan

Your ability to plan and organize every detail of your great business is essential to your success and profitability. *A good business plan must contain values: clear, core principles: Vision: ideal picture of the future of the business, mission: goals to accomplish, purpose: reasons why business exists, excellent leadership and management, excellent products and services, excellent reputation in market and solid financials.*

Crafting a good business plan requires thinking and the quality of your thinking about the key elements of your business has the greatest impact of all on your success and needs you to answer questions like what are the core values and principles that you and your business stand for and believe in? If your business was perfect in every way, what would it look like in future? What is your mission for your business defined in terms of how you would want to change or improve the life or work of your customers? Solid business plans donot necessarily meansuccess. But for Entrepreneurs with decent ideas, they surely boost the odds. A good plan accomplishes three important tasks.

First, it aligns the management team toward a common set of goals. Then, once the vision is on paper, it forces the team to take a long, hard look at the feasibility of the business. "A business plan is like a dry run to see if there is a major problem with your business before losing any money," says Mike McKeever, author of How To Write A Business Plan. Finally, a business plan is a sales document: It aims to attract professional investors who may only have time for a cursory glance at each idea that crosses their desks. Here, then, are some highlights of an effective business plan. Start with a clear, concise executive summary of your business.

Think of it like an elevator pitch. In no more than two pages, billboard all the important stuff. At the top, communicate your value proposition: what your company does, how it will make money and why customers will want to pay for your product or service. If you are sending your plan to investors, include the amount of money you need and how you plan to use it. You have to know the whole picture before you can boil things down, so tackle the summary after finishing the rest of your plan.

Next, establish the market opportunity. Answer questions like: How large is your target market? How fast is it growing? Where are the opportunities and threats, and how will you deal with them? Again, highlight your value proposition. Most of this market information can be found through industry associations, chambers of commerce, census data or even from other business owners. (Be sure to source all of your information in case you are asked to back up your claims or need to update your business plan).

While you may have convinced yourself that your product or service is unique, donot fall into that trap. Instead, get real and size up the competition: Who are they? What do they sell? How much market share do they have? Why will customers choose your product or service instead of theirs? What are the barriers to entry? Remember to include indirect competitors—those with similar capabilities that currently cater to a different market but could choose to challenge you down the road. Now that you have established your idea, start addressing the execution—specifically, your team.

Include profiles of each of your business's founders, partners or officers and what kinds of skills, qualifications and accomplishments they bring to the table. (Include resumes in an appendix.) If potential investors have read this far, it is time to give them the nuts and bolts of your business model. This includes a detailed description of all revenue streams (product sales, advertising, services, licensing) and the company's cost structure (salaries, rent, inventory, maintenance).

Be sure to list all assumptions and provide a justification for them. Also, include names of key suppliers or distribution partners. After all of that, one big question still remains: Exactly how much money does your business stand to make? More important, when will the cash come in the door? That is why you need a section containing past financial performance (if your company is a going concern) and financial projections.

Three-year forward-looking profit-and-loss, balance sheet and cash-flow statements are a must—as is a break-even analysis that shows how much revenue you need to cover your initial investment. For early stage companies with only so much in the Bank, the cash-flow statement comparing quarterly receivables to payables is most critical. "Everyone misunderstands cash flow," says Tim Berry, president of business-plan software company Palo Alto Software. "People think that if they plan for [accounting] profits, they will have cash flow. But many companies that go under are profitable when they die, because profits are not cash." After you have buffed your plan to a shine, donot file it away to gather dust. "A business plan is the beginning of a process," says Berry.

"Planning is like steering, and steering means constantly correcting errors. The plan itself holds just a piece of the value; it is the going back and seeing where you were wrong and why that matters." Further, before coming up with a winning business plan you need to ask yourself the following questions: How long should the business plan be? When should you write it? Who needs a business plan? Why should you write a business plan? After answering these questions,you need to determine your goals and objectives, outline your financing needs, plan what you will do with your plan and of course do not forget about marketing.

A great business plan should consist of the following sections: executive summary within the overall outline of the business plan, the executive summary will follow the title page. The summary should tell the reader what you want. This is very important. All too often, what the business owner desires is buried on page eight. Clearly state what you are asking for in the summary.

Business Description

The business description usually begins with a short description of the industry. When describing the industry, discuss the present outlook as well as future possibilities. You should also provide information on all the various markets within the industry, including any new products or developments that will benefit or adversely affect your business.

Market Strategies

Market strategies are the result of a meticulous market analysis. A market analysis forces the Entrepreneur to become familiar with all aspects of the market so that the target market can be defined and the company can be positioned in order to garner its share of sales.

Competitive Analysis

The purpose of the competitive analysis is to determine the strengths and weaknesses of the competitors within your market, strategies that will provide you with a distinct advantage, the barriers that can be developed in order to prevent competition from entering your market, and any weaknesses that can be exploited within the product development cycle.

Design & Development Plan

The purpose of the design and development plan section is to provide investors with a description of the product's design, chart its development within the context of production, marketing and the company itself, and create a development budget that will enable the company to reach its goals.

Operations & Management Plan

The operations and management plan is designed to describe just how the business functions on a continuing basis. The operations plan will highlight the logistics of the organization such as the various responsibilities of the management team, the tasks assigned to each division within the company, and capital and expense requirements related to the operations of the business.

Financial Factors Financial data is always at the back of the business plan, but that doesn't mean it's any less important than up-front material such as the business concept and the management team.

What Makes a Good Business Plan?

What factors are involved in creating a good business plan? Is it the length of the plan? The information it covers? How well is it written or the brilliance of its strategy. The following illustration shows a business plan as part of a process. You can think about the good or bad of a plan as the plan itself, measuring its value by its contents. There are some qualities in a plan that make it more likely to create results, and these are important.

However, it is even better to see the plan as part of the whole process of results, because even a great plan is wasted if nobody follows it. A business plan will be hard to implement unless it is simple, specific, realistic and complete. Even if it is all these things, a good plan will need someone to follow up and check on it. The plan depends on the human elements around it, particularly the process of commitment and involvement, and the tracking and follow-up that comes afterward.

Successful implementation starts with a good plan. There are elements that will make a business plan more likely to be successfully implemented. Some of the clues to implementation include:

1. **Is the plan simple?** Is it easy to understand and to act on? Does it communicate its contents easily and practically?
2. **Is the plan specific?** Are its objectives concrete and measurable? Does it include specific actions and activities, each with specific date of completion, specific persons responsible and specific budgets?
3. **Is the plan realistic?** Are the sales goals, expense budgets, and milestone dates realistic? Nothing stifles implementation like unrealistic goals.
4. **Is the plan complete?** Does it include all the necessary elements? Requirements of a business plan vary, depending on the context. There is no guarantee, however, that the plan will work if it doesnot cover the main bases.

Too many people think of business plans as something you do to start a company, apply for a loan, or find investors. Yes, they are vital for those purposes, but there is a lot more to it. Preparing a business plan is an organized, logical way to look at all of the important aspects of a business. First, decide what you will use the plan for, such as to: • Define and fix objectives, and programs to achieve those objectives. • Create regular business review and course correction.

Keys to a better business plan

1. Use a business plan to set concrete goals, responsibilities and deadlines to guide your business.
2. A good business plan assigns tasks to people or department
3. A practical business plan includes 10 parts implementation for every one part strategy.
4. As part of the implementation of a business plan, it should provide a forum for regular review and course corrections.
5. Good business plans are practical.
6. Donot use a business plan to show how much you know about your business.
7. Nobody reads a long-winded business plan: not Bankers, bosses, nor venture capitalists. *Years ago, people were favorably impressed by long plans. Today, nobody is interested in a business plan more than 50 pages long.*

CHAPTER 22

Venture Growth Stages

Figure below presents the traditional life- cycle stages of an enterprise. These stages include new venture development, start-up activities, growth, stabilization, and innovation or decline.

Figure Venture Growth Stages

Profitability

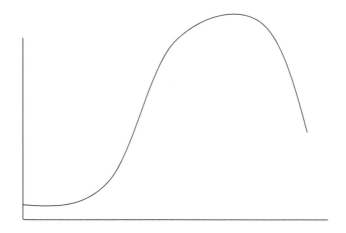

Revenue
New-Venture Venture Business Innovation
Start-up Growth Stabilization or Decline

Source: Ngwira (2015), Development Activities

New venture development

The first stage, new venture development, consists of activities associated with the initial formulation of the venture. This initial phase is the foundation of entrepreneurial process and requires creativity and assessment.

In addition to the accumulation and expansion of resources, this is a creativity, assessment, and networking stage for initial for initial entrepreneurial strategy formulation. Thus, the enterprise general philosophy, mission, scope and direction are determined during this stage.

Startup activities

The second stage, startup activities, encompasses the foundation work for creating a formal business plan, searching for capital, carrying out market activities and developing an effective entrepreneurial team. These activities typically demand an aggressive entrepreneurial strategy with maximum efforts devoted to launching the venture. This stage is similar to chandler's description of rationalization of the use of the firm's resources. Strategic and operational planning steps designed to identify the firm's competitive advantage and operational planning steps designed to identify it. Many business managers say that marketing and financial considerations tend to be paramount during this stage.

Growth

The growth stage often requires major changes in entrepreneurial strategy. Competition and other marketing forces call for the reformation of strategies. For example, some firms find themselves "growing out" of business because they are unable to cope with the growth of their ventures. Many business commentators say that highly creative Entrepreneurs sometimes are unable, or unwilling, to meet the administrative challenges that accompany this growth stage. As a result, they leave the ventures and move on to other ventures. The creative ideas are detrimental to the growth of the venture. The firm needed a managerial Entrepreneur to run the operations: jobs had neither the expertise nor the desire to assume this role.

The growth stage presents newer and more substantial problems than those the Entrepreneur faced during the startup stage. These newer challenges force the entrepreneur into developing step of skills while maintaining an "entrepreneurial perspective" for the organization. Thus, the growth stage is a transition from entrepreneurial one-person leadership to managerial team-oriented leadership

Business Stabilization

Business commentators say that the stabilization stage is a result of both marketing conditions and the entrepreneur's efforts. During this stage a number of developments commonly occur, including increased competition, consumer difference to the Entrepreneur's good(s) or service(s) and situation of the market with a host of "me too" looks-likes. Thus, sales often begin to stabilize and Entrepreneur begins thinking about where the enterprise will go over the next three years. Many writers describe this stage as a swing stage in that it proceeds the period when the firm either swings into higher gear and greater profitability of swings toward decline and failure. During this stage innovations is often critical to future success.

Innovation or Decline

Generally, firms that fail to innovate will die. Financially successful enterprises often will try to acquire other innovative firms, thereby ensuring their own growth. Also, many firms will work on new products/services development.

Why so many businesses fail

According to longitudinal study conducted by Jones (2005), approximately 60% of small businesses shut down within the first six years. Small businesses fail to grow for numerous reasons. The most common reasons are: because their owners: grow their company too fast: have a poor concept: are not good at marketing or sales: fail to plan: start their company without enough money to get to breakeven: have an inability to differentiate: lack control of their finances and books: or donot build systems and processes. Many entrepreneurs who end their finances and books: or donot build systems and processes. Many Entrepreneurs who end up unsuccessful do not build process and systems and lack the ability or desire to sell.

They do not carefully plan their business and often fail to raise the needed capital to sustain it until it is profitable. They do not focus on efficiency of operations or automation. They make the investment in additional capital or employees needed to expand the company to the point where it can make profit. As an Entrepreneur, even if you have a great idea, you will have to plan well, build a long-term team, make sure you have adequate capitalization, build the proper systems, and execute your plan.

According to Entrepreneur and adjunct business professor at UNC's Kenan-Flagler Business School Colin Wahl, there are certain critical success factors in building a successful small business. These include: vision of the management: passion: a good idea: clean, focused business objectives: a well thought through business plan: good organization:enthusiasm in the owners: a good team: motivated employees: good cash flow management: adequate financial resources: a clear understanding of marketing need: and execution of the management.

CHAPTER 23

Competitive Advantage Issues

A competitive advantage is what distinguishes you from the competition in the minds of your customers. Whether you are an employee, a business or a country, you need to have a clear competitive advantage and communicate it to your customers. Before you can determine your competitive advantage, you haveto know these three determinants:

1. **What you produce**. Whether goods or services, you have to be very clear on what you are providing. New technologycan redefine that for you, so you have to constantly stay on top of how trends affect the benefits you provide. For example, the Internet meant that newspapers had to redefine how they delivered the news.

2. **Target market**. Who are your customers? You have to know exactly who buys from you, and how you can make them happier. This increases demand, the driver of all economic growth. Newspapers found out their target market started to become older people, who werenot as comfortable getting their news online.

3. **Competition**. This is not just other similar companies or products, but anything else your customer does to meet their needs. Newspapers thought their competition was other newspapers, until they realized it was the Internet. How could they compete with a news provider that was instant and free?

Once you are clear on these three determinants, then you can decide what benefit you provide better than the competition to your target market.Reinforce that message in every communication to your customers, including advertising, public relations, and even your storefront and employees. If you are the employee, treat yourself as if you were in business for yourself -- because you are. Make sure your competitive advantage is reflected in your appearance, your resume, and in how you communicate.

Sustainable Competitive Advantage

Just because a company is the market leader now, doesnot mean it has a sustainable competitive advantage.A company can temporarily cut its prices to gain market share, but its competitive lead will disappear when it restores those prices to a profitable level. A company must create clear goals, strategies, and operations to sustain its competitive advantage over time. The corporate culture and values of the employees must be in alignment with those goals, as well. It is difficult to do all those things well, which is why very few companies can create a sustainable competitive advantage.

Michael Porter: The Guru of Competitive Advantage

In 1985, Harvard Business School professor Michael Porter wrote the definitive business school textbook on the topic, called *Competitive Advantage*. In it, he outlined the three major ways companies achieve sustainableadvantage: cost leadership, differentiation and focus. Although these main strategies were developed by researching companies, they can be useful for everyone, from employees to countries, who are seeking to stand out.

Cost leadership means you provide reasonable value at a lower price. Companies do this by continuously improving operational efficiency. They usually pay their workers less, either by providing intangible benefits such as stock options, benefits or promotional opportunities, or by taking advantage of unskilled labor surpluses. As they get larger, they can take advantage of economies of scale, and buy in bulk. Good examples of companies with sustainable cost leadership advantage are Walmart and Costco. However, sometimes they pay below the cost of living. Their advantage can be threatened if they must comply with higher minimum wage laws.

Differentiation means you have a strong brand that clearly communicates how you deliver benefits much better than anyone else. A company can achieve differentiation by providing a unique or high-quality product, by delivering it faster, or by marketing it in a way that truly reaches customers better. Instead of being a cost leader, the company with a differentiation strategy can charge a premium price. That means they usually have higher profit margins.

Companies usually achieve differentiation with innovation, quality or customer service. Innovation means you meet the same needs in a new way. A great example of this is Apple. The iPod is innovative because it allows you to play whatever music you want, in any order. Quality means you provide the best product or service, and so might be higher priced. Tiffany's is able to charge more because it's seen as the best. Customer service means going out of the way to delight the customer. Nordstrom's is known for this.

Focus means you understand and service your target market better than anyone else. You can use either a cost leadership or differentiation strategy, but you focus it on one specific target market. Often, it is a tiny niche that isnot being served by larger companies.Community banks are an example of a segment that uses a focus strategy to gain sustainable competitive advantage. They target local, small businesses, or high net worth individuals. Their target audience enjoys the personal touch that big Banks may not be able to give, and they are willing to pay a little more in fees for this service. These Banks are using a differentiation form of the focus strategy.

How Countries Use Competitive Advantage

A country can function in line with a competitive advantage. This is known as national competitive advantage, or comparative advantage. ***For example, China uses cost leadership to export reasonably quality products at a lower price.*** It can do this because its standard of livingis lower, so it can pay its workers less. It also fixes the value of its currency, the yuan, at a lower value than the dollar.

India started as a cost leader, but is moving toward differentiation. It provides skilled technical, English-speaking workers at a reasonable wage. Japan changed its competitive advantage. In the 1960s, it was known for cheap electronics. By the 1980s, it had known for quality brands, such as Sony.

America's comparative advantage is innovation. U.S. companies are able to bring innovative products to market faster and more successfully than other countries. A great example is Silicon Valley, America's innovative advantage.

Competitive advantage deals with areas of specialization. The Entrepreneur should single out which area of specialization he is good at than his competitors. This could be in the area of skills, competencies, talents and abilities. If you do not have competitive advantage then do not compete. The competitive priorities discussed in chapter 13such as quality, speed, dependability, flexibility and cost(doing business cheaply) should be considered. Additionally, there is also need to understand the nature of competition whether it is direct or indirect. Competitor analysis should be done to find out who are the real competitors, what are their strengths and weaknesses, what could be the advantages over them and what makes you unique than them?

Building a Competitive Advantage

The goal of developing a strategic plan is to create for the business a competitive advantage – the aggregation of factors that sets the business apart from its competitors and gives the unique position in the chosen market arena. From a strategic perspective the key to business success is to develop a unique competitive advantage, one that creates value for customers and is difficult for competitors to duplicate.

No business can be everything to everyone. In fact, one of the biggest pitfalls many Entrepreneurs stumble into is failing to differentiate their companies from their crowd of competitors. Entrepreneurs often face the challenge of setting their businesses apart from their larger, more powerful competitors (who can easily outspend them) by using their creativity and special abilities their businesses offer customers.

In the long run a company gains a sustainable competitive advantage through its ability to develop a set of core competencies that enable it to serve its selected target customers better than its rivals.

Core competencies that enable it to serve its selected target customers better than its rivals. Core competencies are a unique set of capabilities that a company develops in key areas, such as superior quality, customer service, innovation, team building, flexibility, responsiveness and others that allow it to vault competitors.

Typically, a company is likely to build core competencies in no more than five or six (sometimes) fewer areas. These core competencies become the nucleus of a company's competitive advantage and are usually quite enduring overtime. Markets, customers and competitors may change but a company's core competencies are more durableforming the building blocks for everything a company does.

To be effective these competencies should be difficult for competitors to duplicate and they must provide customers with some kind of perceived benefit. As stated earlier company's core competencies often have to do with advantages of their size – speed, closeness to their customers, superior service and ability to innovate. The key success is building these core competencies and concentrating them on providing superior service and value for its target customers. However, it should be noted that developing core competencies does not necessarily require a company to spend a great deal of money. It does however require an Entrepreneur to use creativity, imagination and vision to identify those things that it does best and that are most important to its target customers.

Building a company's strategy around its core competencies allows the business to gain a sustainable competitive edge over it rivals and to ride its strategy to victory.

Porter's framework for competitive advantage

Environmental determinants of advantage (Porter, 1991) --

Firms create and sustain competitive advantage because of the capacity to continuously improve, innovate, and upgrade their competitive advantages over time. Upgrading is the process of shifting advantages throughout the value chain to more sophisticated types, and employing higher levels of skill and technology. Successful firms are those that improve and innovate in ways that are valued not only at home but elsewhere.

Competitive success is enhanced by moving early in each product or process generation, provided that the movement is along a path that reflects evolving technology and buyer need, and that early movers subsequently upgrade their positions rather than rest upon them. In this view, firms have considerable discretion in relaxing external and internal constraints.

Four broad attributes of the proximate environment of a firm have the greatest influence on its ability to innovate and upgrade. These attributes shape the information firms have available to perceive opportunities, the pool of inputs, skills and knowledge they can draw upon, the goals that condition investment, and the pressures on the firm to act. The environment is important in providing the initial insight that underpins competitive advantage, the inputs needed to act on it, and to accumulate knowledge and skills over time, and the forces needed to keep progressing.

PART IV

MASTERING WEALTHY CREATION PRINCIPLES

CHAPTER 24

How to Become and Stay Wealthy

The real fact is that we all want to be well off, wealthy, rich and abundant. And we are fascinated by others who already are. The question is how did they do it? How can we do it too? The simple truth is that wealthy people tend to understand and do things the rest of us donot do. From mindsets to casual actions, they follow behavioral rules when it comes to their wealth and these rules are what separate them from everybody else. This chapter codifies what those behaviors are so that you too can choose to be more wealth. The basis of the rules is that these are the things I have observed wealthy people do. This means that if we do like them, we will become like them. This actually does work.

Wealth creation involves knowing what to do to make money, how to carry on making money, how to hang on it once you have got, how to spend, invest and enjoy money and make use of it altruistically. This assumes that you want to get richer, do it legally, do something useful with it once you have got it, put something back, keep some of this stuff under your hat and that you are prepared to put a bit of work. Therefore, this chapter is about thinking wealth, getting wealth, staying wealthy and sharing your wealth. We start with thinking wealth because that is the foundation.

Wealthy Thinking

Money is a concept. You cannot really see or touch it. You can only do that with some physical symbol of it like Bank notes or a cheque. Bits of paper yes but bits of paper with enormous power. The good news about becoming wealthy is that anybody can make money and that this is not selective or discriminatory. You have the same rights and opportunities as everyone else to take as much as you want. Of the wealth the world each has as much as they can make and take. What else could make sense? There is no way money can know who is handling it, what qualifications are, what ambitions they have or what class they belong to. It is very clear that money has no ears or eyes or senses ears. Money is there to be used, spent, saved and invested, fought over, seduced with and worked for it.

Knowledge

Everything you know or believe about money did not come to you at birth. You were conditioned in your attitude towards finance as you grew in your family or environment of your upbringing. Until the knowledge you have of finance is appropriate one for wealthy creation, every plan you have gets messed up by the disjointed opinions you hold. Every time you want to create wealth, you might find at the back of your mind things rising against it, thus, causing you to make excuses and reject what finances are coming your way. So, thinking that money is scarce, evil, bad or dirty will make it hard for money to come to you until you get the right education. Robert Kiyosaki, author of Rich Dad and Poor Dad says there are three forms of education: academic, professional and financial education. People are not wealthy and even go to the extent of being poor because they are financially illiterate. To be financially mis-educated is to use slow words like "I will never be rich". Financial mis-education will teach you to write strong business proposals that will create jobs for others and profit for companies and not have to create something for your future.

Multiplying money is a skill and requires that you be adequately informed and continue to inform yourself on how to make money and see it increase. You must ask yourself how you will put your brain to work instead of asking how you can afford things. Wealth creation rests in educating your mind and you need to know that being broke and being poor are not the same because if you are broke it is a temporary thing but poverty is eternal. You must educate yourself to know that multiplying money is necessary because money is a form of power and once you have it you have the ability to respond.

Dedication

Dedication and commitment are the next steps after acquiring financial knowledge. Commitment must be put into action by crafting a game plan. Wealthy people would not have become who they are by chance but by taking tangible actions.

If you are to leave where you are to where you ought to be, there must be a clear description of the map. You have got to have a plan. The plan gives you the important bit – how you are going to get there. This is a function of strategic vision which is a description of the road map. This type of thinking will make you to put your heart and soul into your assignment which will create wealth for you.

Investment

Many business commentators say that investment simply means the science of money-making. This means that once your commitment towards creation is established the next thing is to start the journey in investment. This is important because you cannot become wealthy only by looking wealthy.

This is a call to develop the ability to multiplying money. With most people, when money gets into their hands, it reduces in quantity. But with some, it multiplies when it reaches their hands. Financial success and wealthy are not all about spending money; it is about making money. The major problem is that most of us were not taught how to make money in schools. Most of our money habits were picked up from our home. We learn how to spend money and not how to make money. The man with five talents traded with what he was given.

This is amazing. If you are in your 20s and 30s and you do not want to be broke at the age of 70, do something now. It is almost too late to start when you turn sixty. Your money habits today determines your financial future. However, financial success is progressive. Until you can manage the hundreds you have, you are not prepared to handle the thousands, then millions and then billions. It is progressive. Until you pass the test on this level, God will not allow you to advance to the next level. He says:God predicts that what you will do with the millions by what you do with the thousands. Money will always flow away from those who do not know how to treat it well to those who know how to treat it well. Different ways to invest include leveraging, treasury bills, investing in stocks, bonds, general business, mutual trust funds, real estate and investing in financial institutions such as Banks.That is the minimum, the least. Here we cannot talk about the savings account. The interest you earn from the savings account is not multiplication. It is a reduction of your money. By the time you factor in inflation at the end of one year and add interest on it, you will realize that the rate of inflation is higher than the interest your money is earning hence you would have lost money in real terms. From today you will not be on the losing end but on the prospering side.

How to be Wealthy

Riches require that you have enough money. But wealth goes further. It is having enough of all the essential of life such as love, good health, friends and family, spiritually and of course, enough money. What we are saying is that being wealthy is a total package – laughter, love, living, good healthy, peace, money and relationships.

The following are proven ways on how you can become wealthy: wealthy thinking; developing an understanding of the power of small and big savings; spending less than you earn; always paying yourself first; saving something out of each dollar; being responsible for where you are in life; paying cash and use less credit; buy stocks not product; keeping track of your money; study and admire the successful in your chosen assignment or field; recognize the difference between income statement

wealthy and balance sheet wealth; do not confuse between debt and wealthy; invest in right ground; form new habits which encourage you in the direction of becoming wealthy for God; set financial goals and assess them; refuse to be stressed; make conscious decision to handle your money matters yourself; create your own entity; become finically literate and give generously.

How to Stay Wealthy

To maintain or sustain wealth is a skill and it requires commitment to the proven wealth principles. It is a matter of following the rules of the game. *It goes without saying that those that love rules will be rulers and those that love commandments will be in command.*

To stay wealthy requires you to follow certain rules. Here are the rules: donot spend it before you have got it; put something aside for your old age – no more than that; put something aside for emergencies or rainy days – this the contingency fund; never borrow money from friends or family but you can allow them to invest; do not surrender equity; know when to stop; never lend money to a friend unless you are prepared to write off; find ways to give people money without them feeling they are in your debt and lastly share your wealth.

Sharing wealth simply means using wealth wisely. Those who abuse their wealth donot tend to stay wealthy for long.Sharing wealth is the same as giving. *We are not to be mere reservoirs that hold on to the blessing, but those who will pass it for others too to enjoy. When God called Abraham, He said He would bless him to be a blessing to his generation.*The process of giving and receiving is what makes the cycle of life to be perpetuated and be enjoyable. Those that keep to themselves do not increase. *There is that scatterth and yet increaseth and there is that with holdeth more than is meet but it tendereth to poverty* **(Proverbs 11:24).**

CHAPTER 25

❧

The Importance of Entrepreneurs to Wealth Creation

The system of entrepreneurship is supposed to foster the spirit of entrepreneurship. In fact, the future of such countries is independent on Entrepreneurs and become the economic power due to entrepreneurial activity. The future of any nation will be greatly influenced by Entrepreneurs with their unique and innovative ideas. Thus, Entrepreneurs are motivated and inspired individuals willing to accept risk and seize opportunities to harness and use resources in novel ways.

The Entrepreneur is the catalysis that brings together the resources of land, labor, and capital to create valuable goods and services and in the hopes of building a profitable business. As stated earlier *the word Entrepreneur is of French origin and derives from entreprendre, which means 'to undertake.' The American heritage dictionary defines an entrepreneur as "a person who organizes, operates, and assumes the risk for a business venture.*

The Entrepreneur plays a vital role in society. Without Entrepreneurs, there would be no businesses, no inventions, no innovations, no progress, and no wealth. Without the Entrepreneur and the system that provides incentives for Entrepreneurs, we would have no printing press, no bifocals, no airplane, no air conditioner, no radio, no micro wave, no computer, no telephone, no television, and no George Foreman Lean Mean Fat Burning Grilling Machine

In short, the standard of living would not be much better than that of 1450. The world would not be able to support the 6.5 billion person it does, and the doomsday Malthusian predictions of overpopulation would have been realized many decades, if not centuries ago. Entrepreneurs develop new markets. Under the modern concept of marketing, markets are people who are willing and able to satisfy their needs. In economics, this is called effective demand.

Entrepreneurs are different from ordinary businessmen who only perfume traditional functions of management like planning organization, and coordination. According to Peters (2008) Entrepreneurs discover new sources of materials. This means that Entrepreneurs are never satisfied with traditional or existing sources of materials to improve their enterprise in terms of supply, cost and quality. Nellis 2007 says that Entrepreneurs mobilize capital resources. David (2010) concurs with Nellis (2012) views by mentioning that Entrepreneurs are the organizers and coordinators of the major factors of production, such as land, labour and capital. This means that they properly mix these factors of production to create goods and service. Lash (2010) argues that capital resources, from a layman's view, refer to money.

However, these views are counter argued by Gerson (2008) who states that capital resources represent machine, buildings and other physical production resources. Therefore, Entrepreneurshave initiatives and self-confidence in accumulating and mobilization capital resources for new business or business expansions.Entrepreneurs introduces new technologies, new industries and new products. Aside from being innovators and reasonable takers, Entrepreneurs take advantage of business opportunities, and transform these into profits. They introduce something new or something different. Such entrepreneurial spirit has greatly contributed to the modernization of the economy. Every year, there are new technologies and new products. All of these are intended to satisfy human needs in more convenient and pleasant way.

Entrepreneurs create employment. Factories, services industries, agricultural enterprise, and the numerous small- scale business provide millions of jobs. Such massive employment has multiplier and accelerator in the whole economy. More jobs mean more income. This increases demand for goods and services. In addition, this stimulates production. Again, more production requires more employment.

Have you ever wondered why some countries are relatively wealthier and others poor? Economists have been studying the issue of wealth creation for many years. They began the process by revealing potential sources of wealth to determine which are the most important. Overtime they came up with five factors that seemed to contribute to wealth. They called them **factors of production.**

These are

1. Land (natural resources)
2. labour (workers)
3. Capital (this includes machines, tools, buildings or whatever else is used in production of goods. It does not include money; money is used to buy factors of production – it is not a factor itself.)
4. Entrepreneurship
5. Knowledge

Traditionally, business and economic textbooks have emphasized only four factors of production: land, labour, capital and entrepreneurship. But management expert and business consultant Peter Drucker says that the important factor of production is and always will be knowledge.If you were to analyze rich countries versus poor countries to see what causes the differences in the levels of wealth, you would have to look at the factors of production in each country. Such analyses have revealed that some relatively poor countries often have plenty of land and natural resources.

Most poor countries have many labourers, so it is not labour that is the primary source of wealth today. Labourers need to find work to contribute to an economy; that is, they need Entrepreneurs to provide jobs for them. Furthermore capital – machinery and tools – is now becoming available in world markets, so capital isnot the missing ingredient. Capital is not productive without Entrepreneurs to put it into use.

Clearly, then what makes rich countries rich today is a contribution of entrepreneurship and the effective use of knowledge. Together, lack of entrepreneurship and the absence of knowledge among workers, along with the lack of freedom, contribute to keeping poor countries poor. The box called Reaching Beyond Our Borders discusses the importance of freedom to economic development.

Entrepreneurship also makes some countries rich while others remain relatively poor. The business environment either encourages or discourages entrepreneurship. In the following chapter, we will explore what makes up the business environment and how to build an environment that encourages growth and job creation.

CHAPTER 26

Things You Did Not Know About Successful Wealthy Entrepreneurs

Where is the wealth to a nation?

Questions such as the above yield important insights into the prospects for sustainable development in countries around the world. The estimates of total wealth – including produced, natural and human and institutional capital – suggest that human capital and the value of institutions (as measured by law) constitute the largest share of wealth in virtually all countries. It is striking that natural capital constitutes quarter of total wealth in suggests that better management of ecosystems and natural resources will be key to sustaining development while these countries build their infrastructure and human institutional capacity. Particularly noteworthy is the share of cropland and pastureland in the natural wealth of poor countries – at 70 percent, this argues for a strong focus on efforts to sustain soil quality.

This new approach to capital also provides a comprehensive measure of changes inwealth, a key indicator of sustainability. There are important examples of resource-dependent countries, such as Botswana, that have used their natural resources to underpin impressive rates of growth. Additionally, the research finds that the value of natural capital per person actually tends to rise with income when we look across countries – this contradicts the received wisdom that development necessarily entails the depletion of the environment. However, the figures suggest that, per capita, most low-income countries have experienced declines in both total and natural capital. This is bad news not only from an environmental point of view, but also from a broader development perspective.

Five Things You Need Know About the Wealthy Entrepreneurs

1. The successful wealthy entrepreneurs are comfortable being uncomfortable

Most people just want to be comfortable. Physical, psychological and emotional comfort is the primary goal of the middle – class mindset. The wealth on the other hand, learn early on that becoming a millionaire isnot easy and the need for comfort can be devastating. They learn to be comfortable while operating in a state of going uncertainty.

The great ones know there is a price to pay for getting rich, but if they have the mental toughness to endure temporary pain, they can reap the harvest of abundant wealth. It is not comfortable for a millionaire in the making to forge ahead when everyone around her is negative, cynical and supportive, yet those who can push forward are rewarded with riches for the rest of their lives. Make a list of the five things you must do today that are uncomfortable but will help you build your financial fortune. Wealth people have goals and plans to meet those objectives.

2. The successful wealthy entrepreneurs dream about the future

The wealthy are future oriented and optimistic about what lies ahead. They appreciate and learn from the past while living in the present and dreaming of the future. Self-made millionaires get rich because they are willing to bet on themselves and project their dreams, goals and ideas into an unknown future. Much of their planning time is spent clarifying goals that won't be realized for years, yet they patiently and painstakingly plan and dream of what their future will look and feel like.

3. The successful wealthy entrepreneurs are more confident

The negative projections and derogatory labels on the rich are endless. One of the most common is that the rich are cocky, arrogant people who think they are better than everyone else. The truth is that successful people are confident because they repeatedly bet on themselves and are rarely disappointed. Even when they fail, they are confident in their ability to learn from the loss and come back stronger and richer than ever. This is not arrogance, but self-assuredness in its finest form.

The wealthy have an elevated and fearless consciousness that keeps them moving toward what they want as opposed to moving away from what they donot want. This often doubles or triples their net worth quickly because of the new efficiency in their thinking and this becomes a self-fulfilling prophecy. *As they move from success to success, they create a psychological tidal wave of momentum that gets stronger every day, catapulting their confidence to a level so high it is often interpreted as arrogance.*

4. The Wealthy Entrepreneurs Believe Money is About Freedom

Among the many money issues misperceived by the general public is the notion that acquiring great wealth is more about showing off than creating choices. While money certainly brings status, it is acquired mostly for the purpose of attaining personal liability. It is impossible to be truly without wealth. *The middle class is controlled by employment, government and other entities with superior resources that dictate what they can and cannot do.* It is tough to make a moral stand for freedom when you are worried about making your next mortgage payment.

Rich people can afford to stand up and fight oppression. They can afford to buy their way out of unhealthy work environments, bad bosses, and other unpleasant situations. They have the means to enlist the doctors when they get sick and they are able to make themselves comfortable as possible when they cannot get well. When they want to raise money for business, politics or charity a few phone calls to their rich friends is what it takes. Start thinking the freedoms you will gain when you are wealthy. Remember like attracts like and rich attracts rich.

5. The Wealthy Entrepreneurs Carefully Monitor their Associations

People with high level formal education like to associate with academic elite. Physically fit people enjoy spending time with others who are fit. Religious people like to have fellowship with people of faith. And rich people like to associate with others who are rich. Like attracts like yet the wealthy are often criticized for having closed inner circle that is almost impossible to break into unless you are rich. ***Successful people generally agree that consciousness is contagious and that exposure to people who are more successful has the potential to expand your thinking and catapult your income.*** We become like the people we associate with and that is why winners are attracted to winners. Set a goal to double the amount of time you spend with people who are richer than you. Who knows, it might just make you rich.

The difference between Income and Wealth

Many economic and business commentators on one hand say that income is a flow of money that goes into factors of production. This include: Wages and salaries paid to people from their jobs; money paid to people receiving welfare benefits such as pension; profits flowing to people who own and lease property; rental income flowing to people who own and lease out property and interest paid to those who hold money in deposit accounts or who own bonds.

On the other hand, economic and business commentators say that wealth is a stock concept. It is a large amount of money or valuable possessions and can be held in different ways: savings held in bank deposits; ownership of shares issued by listed companies and equity stakes in private businesses; the ownership of property; wealth held in bonds and wealth held in occupational pension schemes and life assurance schemes. Wealth generates income for if you have built up savings balances they ought to pay interest

Many Dimensions of Poverty

A plethora of definitions of poverty have emerged. Poverty is hunger. Poverty is lack of shelter. Poverty is being sick and not being able to see a doctor. Poverty is not having access to school and not knowing how to read. Poverty is not having a job and is fear for the future, living one day at a time. Poverty is powerlessness, lack of representation and freedom. The prosperity of each individual constitutes the wealth of the nation which eventually help to finance the public sector.

CHAPTER 27

Mastering the Business Model: Revenue, Profits and Costs

Why Are Cost, Revenue & Profit Important?

Cost, revenue and profit are the three most important factors in determining the success of your business. A business can have high revenue, but if the costs are higher, it will show no profit and is destined to go out of business when available capital runs out. Managing costs and revenue to maximize profit is key for any entrepreneur.

Definition of Terms

Revenue is the same as total income for a business and measures all money taken in through sales of goods and services. Cost measures the total expenditures made by the business to run the operation: both the "direct" costs involved in creating the goods or services, as well as the "indirect" costs that stem from running a business, such as rent, salaries and legal or professional fees. *Profit is the total revenue minus the total cost; this is the money made by the business and is the key indicator of success.*

Revenues vs. Profit

Many businesses are judged on the basis of revenues, not profit. For example, an Internet startup may show high revenues even in the early stages of the business but will typically spend far more money than total revenue on business expansion and marketing. This is only possible when investors are available to provide additional capital -- the term for investment money provided to the business -- that allows it to spend more money than it brings in. In the long run, a business that requires constant investment will fail; only a profitable business will be able to pay back its investors. Sometimes, however, an Entrepreneur may be able to personally succeed if he can sell his business while it is unprofitable, if investors believe the chance of future profitability is high. In most cases, however, only profitable businesses can be sold at reasonable prices to new owners.

Cost Reduction

Everything a business spends money on is a cost, and many businesses attempt to increase their profitability by reducing costs. There are many sound ways to do this; for example, a retail business can expand by starting additional stores or can take the much cheaper option of starting an online business to complement its brick-and-mortar operation. However, some methods of reducing costs will be damaging to the business: Pay your employees too little or reduce your staff too much, and you will be unable to handle enough sales to generate future profits.

Profit Measurement

Good Entrepreneurs measure their profitability very frequently, perhaps on a daily basis. All goods sold must be priced high enough above cost to pay for the direct costs spent to acquire or create the good, as well as their share of overall indirect costs. When costs of goods increase, their price must increase as well, or the product must be dropped from the product line. A strong business may offer regular sales or bargain pricing to move customers into the stores, but no business can survive if the pricing of individual goods or services does not consistently return profits back into the business.

Cost–volume–profit analysis

Cost–volume–profit (**CVP**), in managerial economics, is a form of cost accounting. It is a simplified model, useful for elementary instruction and for short-run decisions.

Overview

A critical part of CVP analysis is the point where total revenues equal total costs (both fixed and variable costs). At this break-even point, a company will experience no income or loss. This break-even point can be an initial examination that precedes more detailed CVP analysis.

CVP analysis employs the same basic assumptions as in breakeven analysis. The assumptions underlying CVP analysis are:

- The behavior of both costs and revenues are linear throughout the relevant range of activity. (This assumption precludes the concept of volume discounts on either purchased materials or sales.)
- Costs can be classified accurately as either fixed or variable.
- Changes in activity are the only factors that affect costs.
- All units produced are sold (there is no ending finished goods inventory).
- When a company sells more than one type of product, the product mix (the ratio of each product to total sales) will remain constant.

The components of CVP analysis are:

- Level or volume of activity
- Unit selling prices
- Variable cost per unit
- Total fixed costs

Assumptions

CVP assumes the following:

- Constant sales price;
- Constant variable cost per unit;
- Constant total fixed cost;
- Units sold equal units produced.

These are simplifying, largely linearizing assumptions, which are often implicitly assumed in elementary discussions of costs and profits. In more advanced treatments and practice, costs and revenue are nonlinear and the analysis is more complicated, but the intuition afforded by linear CVP remains basic and useful.

One of the main methods of calculating CVP is profit–volume ratio which is (contribution /sales)*100 = this gives us profit–volume ratio.

- contribution stands for sales minus variable costs.

Therefore it gives us the profit added per unit of variable costs.

Model

The assumptions of the CVP model yield the following linear equations for total costs and total revenue (sales):

Total cost = fixed costs + (unit variable cost x number of units)

Total revenue = sales price x number of units

These are linear because of the assumptions of constant costs and prices, and there is no distinction between units produced and units sold, as these are assumed to be equal. Note that when such a chart is drawn, the linear CVP model is assumed, often implicitly.

In symbols:

$$TC = TFC + V \times X$$
$$TR = P \times X$$

where

- TC= Total costs
- TFC= Total fixed costs
- V = Unit variable cost (variable cost per unit)
- X = Number of units
- TR = S = Total revenue = Sales
- P= (Unit) sales price

Profit is computed as TR-TC; it is a profit if positive, a loss if negative.

Break down

Costs and sales can be broken down, which provide further insight into operations.

One can decompose total costs as fixed costs plus variable costs:

$$TC = TFC + V \times X$$

Following a matching principle of matching a portion of sales against variable costs, one can decompose sales as contribution plus variable costs, where **contribution** is "what's left after deducting variable costs". One can think of contribution as "the marginal contribution of a unit to the profit", or "contribution towards offsetting fixed costs".

In symbols:

$$
\begin{aligned}
TR \quad &= P \times X \\
&= (\, (P - V) + V \,) \times X \\
&= (\, C + V \,) \times X
\end{aligned}
$$

$$= C \times V + V \times X$$

where

- **C = Unit Contribution (Margin)**

Subtracting variable costs from both costs and sales yields the simplified diagram and equation for profit and loss.

In symbols:

$$
\begin{aligned}
\text{PL} \ &= \text{TR} - \text{TC} \\
&= (C + V) \times X - (\text{TFC} + V \times X) \\
&= C \times X - \text{TFC}
\end{aligned}
$$

Fig. Sales, Profit and Total Costs

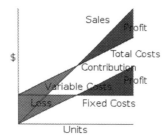

Source: Ngwira (2015), quantities in CVP.

These graphs can be related by a rather busy diagram, which demonstrates how if one subtracts variable costs, the sales and total costs lines shift down to become the contribution and fixed costs lines. Note that the profit and loss for any given number of unit sales is the same, and in particular the break-even point is the same, whether one computes by sales = total costs or as contribution = fixed costs. Mathematically, the contribution graph is obtained from the sales graph by a shear, to be precise where V are unit variable costs.

Applications

CVP simplifies the computation of breakeven in break-even analysis, and more generally allows simple computation of target income sales. It simplifies analysis of short run trade-offs in operational decisions.

Limitations

CVP is a short run, marginal analysis: it assumes that unit variable costs and unit revenues are constant, which is appropriate for small deviations from current production and sales, and assumes a neat division between fixed costs and variable costs, though in the long run all costs are variable. For longer-term analysis that considers the entire life-cycle of a product, one therefore often prefers activity-based costing or throughput accounting.

When we analyze CVP is where we demonstrate the point at which in a firm there will be no profit nor loss means that firm works in breakeven situation. For example:

1. Segregation of total costs into its fixed and variable components is always a daunting task to do. 2. Fixed costs are unlikely to stay constant as output increases beyond a certain range of activity. 3. The analysis is restricted to the relevant range specified and beyond that the results can become unreliable.

4. Aside from volume, other elements like inflation, efficiency, capacity and technology impact on costs

5. Impractical to assume sales mix remain constant since this depends on the changing demand levels.

6. The assumption of linear property of total cost and total revenue relies on the assumption that unit variable cost and selling price are always constant. In real life it is valid within relevant range or period and likely to change

When Talking About Business Models, Remember That Profits Equal Revenues Minus Costs

There is no shortage of discussion about Internet business models these days. And they almost always focus on revenues. But revenues are only half of the value creation equation. The other half is costs.

Let me explain. Businesses are worth the net present value of future cash flows. Cash flows means profits basically (capital expenditures are important but I am going to leave them out of the discussion on this post). So, a business is worth the sum of all of its future profits, discounted back to a net present value. For those who donot want a lesson in finance, you can simplify this theory even more by using a cash flow multiple as a proxy for a net present value. I like to use a 10x multiple for cash flow as a simplistic proxy for net present value.

So, with that simplification, the value of a business is approximated by 10 x (revenues – costs). You can focus on creating value by driving revenues or you can focus on creating value by driving profits. And they are not the same. Because costs donot have to grow linearly with revenues.

How to Forecast Revenue and Growth

When starting out, financial forecasts may seem overwhelming. We will help you conquer the numbers with this easy-to-follow guide to forecasting revenues and expenses during startup. Forecasting business revenue and expenses during the startup stage is really more of an art than a science. Many Entrepreneurs complain that building forecasts with any degree of accuracy takes a lot of time that could be spent selling rather than planning. But few investors will put money in your business if you are unable to provide a set of thoughtful forecasts. More important, proper financial forecasts will help you develop operational and staffing plans that will help make your business a success.

Here is some detail on how to go about building financial forecasts when you are just getting your business off the ground and do not have the luxury of experience.

1. Start with expenses, not revenues. When you are in the startup stage, it is much easier to forecast expenses than revenues. So, start with estimates for the most common categories of expenses as follows:

Fixed Costs/Overhead

- Rent
- Utility bills
- Phone bills/communication costs
- Accounting/bookkeeping
- Legal/insurance/licensing fees
- Postage
- Technology
- Advertising & marketing
- Salaries

Variable Costs

- Cost of Goods Sold

  - o Materials and supplies
  - o Packaging

- Direct Labor Costs

  - o Customer service
  - o Direct sales
  - o Direct marketing

Here are some rules of thumb you should follow when forecasting expenses:

- Double your estimates for advertising and marketing costs since they always escalate beyond expectations.

- Triple your estimates for legal, insurance and licensing fees since they are very hard to predict without experience and almost always exceed expectations.
- Keep track of direct sales and customer service time as a direct labor expense even if you are doing these activities yourself during the startup stage because you will want to forecast this expense when you have more clients.

2. Forecast revenues using both a conservative case and an aggressive case. If you are like most Entrepreneurs, you will constantly fluctuate between conservative reality and an aggressive dream state which keeps you motivated and helps you inspire others. I call this dream state "audacious optimism."

Rather than ignoring the audacious optimism and creating forecasts based purely on conservative thinking, I recommend that you embrace your dreams and build at least one set of projections with aggressive assumptions. You won't become big unless you think big! By building two sets of revenue projections (one aggressive, one conservative), you will force yourself to make conservative assumptions and then relax some of these assumptions for your aggressive case.

For example, your conservative revenue projections might have the following assumptions:

- Low price point
- Two marketing channels
- No sales staff
- One new product or service introduced each year for the first three years

Your aggressive case might have the following assumptions

- Low price point for base product, higher price for premium product
- Three to four marketing channels managed by you and a marketing manager
- Two salespeople paid on commission

- One new product or service introduced in the first year, five more products or services introduced for each segment of the market in years two and three

By unleashing the power of thinking big and creating a set of ambitious forecasts, you are more likely to generate the breakthrough ideas that will grow your business.

3. Check the key ratios to make sure your projections are sound. After making aggressive revenue forecasts, it is easy to forget about expenses. Many Entrepreneurs will optimistically focus on reaching revenue goals and assume the expenses can be adjusted to accommodate reality if revenue doesnot materialize. The power of positive thinking might help you grow sales, but it is not enough to pay your bills!

The best way to reconcile revenue and expense projections is by a series of reality checks for key ratios. Here are a few ratios that should help guide your thinking:

4. Gross margin

What is the ratio of total direct costs to total revenue during a given quarter or given year? This is one of the areas in which aggressive assumptions typically become too unrealistic. Beware of assumptions that make your gross margin increase from 10 to 50 percent. If customer service and direct sales expenses are high now, they will likely be high in the future.

5. Operating profit margin

What is the ratio of total operating costs--direct costs and overheard, excluding financing costs--to total revenue during a given quarter or given year? You should expect positive movement with this ratio. As revenues grow, overhead costs should represent a small proportion of total costs and your operating profit margin should improve. The mistake that many Entrepreneurs make is they forecast this break-even point too early and assume they won't need much financing to reach this point.

6. Total headcount per client

If you are a one-man-army Entrepreneur who plans to grow the business on your own, pay special attention to this ratio. Divide the number of employees at your company--just one if you are a jack-of-all-trades--by the total number of clients you have. Ask yourself if youwant to be managing that many accounts in five years when the business has grown. If not, you will need to revisit your assumptions about revenue or payroll expenses or both.

Building an accurate set of growth projections for your startup will take time. When I first started my company, I avoided building a detailed set of projections because I knew the business model would evolve and change. But I regret not spending more time on business planning since I would have avoided several expenses along the way. The company's board of directors now requires me to prepare quarterly updates to our financial projections. Now when I lapse into fits of audacious optimism, the projections force me to forecast what these dreams mean for the company's bottom line.

Part V

HARVESTING A DOG BUSINESS

CHAPTER 28

Retrenchment

Be passionate in your giving to encounter high harvests

In this chapter we will look at one of harvesting strategies. This is retrenchment. Harvesting is most often referring to selling a business or product line, as when a company sells a product line or division or a family sells a business. Harvesting is also occasionally used to refer to sales of a product or product line towards the end of a product life cycle. Harvesting is therefore a strategy in which investment in a particular line of business is reduced or eliminated because the revenue brought in by additional investment would not warrant the expense. A harvest strategy is employed when a line of business is considered to be a cash cow, meaning that the brand is mature and is unlikely to grow if more investment is added

The company will instead siphon off the revenue that the cash cow brings in until the brand is no longer profitable. Simply put harvesting is the final phase in the entrepreneurial value creation process, which includes building, growing, and harvesting. Harvesting is the process Entrepreneurs and Investors use to exit a business and liquidate their investment in a firm. While all three phases are important pieces of the entrepreneurial process, many Entrepreneurs who fail to execute a successful harvest do not realize the full benefits of their years of labor.

Harvesting is the means for capturing or unlocking value, reducing risk, and creating exit options. It is about more than money, as it also involves personal and non-financial considerations. As a consequence, even upon realizing an acceptable monetary value for the firm, an Entrepreneur who is not prepared for the lifestyle transition that accompanies the harvest may come away disappointed with the overall outcome. Thus, crafting a harvest strategy is as essential to the Entrepreneur's personal success as it is to his or her financial success. The message to the Entrepreneur is this: the time to develop an effective harvest strategy is now, not later. As a firm moves toward the harvest, two questions regarding value are of primary importance. First, are the current owners/managers creating value? You can harvest only what you have created.

Retrenchment

All businesses that reach the decline stage and they cannot be innovated they must be retrenched. Normally such businesses are called dogs because they have a low market share and low market growth. They are a cash drain. Therefore, retrenchment is a strategy that businesses use to reduce diversity or overall size of the operations. The main aim of this strategy is to cut expenses with a goal of becoming financial stable.

Different Types of Retrenchment Strategies

1. Turn around Strategies

Turnaround strategy means backing out, withdrawing or retreating from a decision wrongly taken earlier in order to reverse the process of decline. There are certain conditions or indicators which point out that a turnaround is needed if the organization has to survive. The following are the danger signs:

- Continuous Losses
- Declining Market Share
- Deterioration in physical facilities
- Surplus Skills Inventory
- Uncompetitive products or services
- Divestment Strategies

2. Liquidation Strategies

Liquidation strategy means closing down the entire firm and selling its assets. It is considered the most extreme and the last resort because it leads to serious consequences such as loss of employment to employees, termination of opportunities where a firm could pursue any future activities and the stigma of failure.

Generally, it is seen that small – scale units, proprietorship firms and partnership liquidate frequently but companies rarely liquidate. Liquidation strategy may be unpleasant as strategic alternative but when a business becomes a dog it is a good proposition. Liquidation strategy may be difficult to find buyers for the business. Moreover, the firm cannot expect adequate compensation. Most reasons for liquidation include:

- Business becoming unprofitable.
- High competition
- Failure of strategy
- Industry overcapacity
- Obsolescence of product process

CHAPTER 29

Divestment

*The grass withers, the flower fades, but the
word of our God stands forever.*

DIVESTMENT is a form of retrenchment strategy used by businesses
when they downsize the scope of their business activities. Divestment
usually involves eliminating a portion of a business. Firms may elect to
sell, close, or spin-off a strategic business unit, major operating division, or
product line. This move often is the final decision to eliminate unrelated,
unprofitable, or unmanageable operations. Divestment is commonly the
consequence of a growth strategy.

Much of the corporate downsizing has been the result of acquisitions
and takeovers. Firms often acquired other businesses with operations in
areas with which the acquiring firm had little experience. After trying
for a number of years to integrate the new activities into the existing
organization, many firms have elected to divest themselves of portions of
the business in order to concentrate on those activities in which they had
a competitive advantage.

Reasons to Divest

In most cases it is not immediately obvious that a unit should be
divested. Many times, management will attempt to increase investment as
a means of giving the unit an opportunity to turn its performance around.
Portfolio models such as the Boston Consulting Group (BCG) Model or
General Electric's Business Screen can be used to identify operations in
need of divestment. For example, products or business operations identified
as "dogs" in the BCG Model are prime candidates for divestment.

Decisions to divest may be made for a number of reasons:

Market Share Too Small: Firms may divest when their market share is too small for them to be competitive or when the market is too small to provide the expected rates of return.

Availability of Better Alternatives: Firms may also decide to divest because they see better investment opportunities. Organizations have limited resources. They are often able to divert resources from a marginally profitable line of business to one where the same resources can be used to achieve a greater rate of return.

Need for Increased Investment: Firms sometimes reach a point where continuing to maintain an operation is going to require large investments in equipment, advertising, research and development, and so forth to remain viable. Rather than invest the monetary and management resources, firms may elect to divest that portion of the business.

Lack of Strategic Fit: A common reason for divesting is that the acquired business is not consistent with the image and strategies of the firm. This can be the result of acquiring a diversified business. It may also result from decisions to restructure and refocus the existing business. Legal Pressures to Divest Firms may be forced to divest operations to avoid penalties for restraint of trade.

Implementation of Divestment Strategies: Firms may pursue a divestment strategy by spinning off a portion of the business and allowing it to operate as an independent business entity. Firms may also divest by selling a portion of the business to another organization. Another way to implement a divestment decision is to simply close a portion of the firm's operations.

Many divestments are blocked by management's expectations for the operation. Firms may expect demand for the product to pick up. Management may also see the poor performance as a temporary setback that can be overcome with time and patience. Decisions to divest a business may be seen as an admission of failure on the part of management and may lead to escalating commitment to the struggling business as a way of protecting management's ego and public image.

Divestment is not usually the first choice of strategy for a business. However, as product demand changes and firms alter their strategies, there will almost always be some portion of the business that is not performing to management's expectations. Such an operation is a prime target for divestment and may well leave the company in a stronger competitive position if it is diveste

CHAPTER 30

Succession Planning

Succession planning is a process for identifying and developing internal people with the potential to fill key business leadership positions in the company. Succession planning increases the availability of experienced and capable employees that are prepared to assume these roles as they become available. Taken narrowly, "replacement planning" for key roles is the heart of succession planning. Effective succession or talent-pool management concerns itself with building a series of feeder groups up and down the entire leadership pipeline or progression. In contrast, replacement planning is focused narrowly on identifying specific backup candidates for given senior management positions.

For the most part position-driven replacement planning (often referred to as the "truck scenario") is a forecast, which research indicates does not have substantial impact on outcomes. Fundamental to the succession-management process is an underlying philosophy that argues that top talent in the corporation must be managed for the greater good of the enterprise. Merck and other companies argue that a "talent mindset" must be part of the leadership culture for these practices to be effective.

Succession planning is a process whereby an organization ensures that employees are recruited and developed to fill each key role within the company. Through your succession planning process, you recruit superior employees, develop their knowledge, skills, and abilities, and prepare them for advancement or promotion into ever more challenging roles. Actively pursuing succession planning ensures that employees are constantly developed to fill each needed role. As your organization expands, loses key employees, provides promotional opportunities, and increases sales, your succession planning guarantees that you have employees on hand ready and waiting to fill new roles.

According to a 2006 Canadian Federation of Independent Business survey, slightly more than one third of independent business owners plan to exit their business as part of harvesting within the next 5 years and within the next 10 years two-thirds of owners plan to exit their business. The survey also found that small and medium sized enterprises are not adequately prepared for their business succession: only 10% of owners have a formal, written succession plan; 38% have an informal, unwritten plan; and the remaining 52% do not have any succession plan at all.

The results are backed by a 2004 CIBC survey which suggests that succession planning is increasingly becoming a critical issue. By 2010, CIBC estimates that $1.2 trillion in business assets are poised to change hands. Research indicates many succession-planning initiatives fall short of their intent (Corporate Leadership Council, 1998). "Bench strength," as it is commonly called, remains a stubborn problem in many if not most companies. Studies indicate that companies that report the greatest gains from succession planning feature high ownership by the CEO and high degrees of engagement among the larger leadership team. Research indicates that clear objectives are critical to establishing effective succession planning.

These objectives tend to be core to many or most companies that have well-established practices: identify those with the potential to assume greater responsibility in the organization; provide critical development experiences to those that can move into key roles; engage the leadership in supporting the development of high-potential leaders; build a data base that can be used to make better staffing decisions for key jobs; In other companies these additional objectives may be embedded in the succession process; improve employee commitment and retention; meet the career development expectations of existing employees and Counter the increasing difficulty and costs of recruiting employees externally.

Succession Planning with Your Board

Succession planning is a means for an organization to ensure its continued effective performance through leadership continuity. For an organization to plan for the replacement of key leaders, potential leaders must first be identified and prepared to take on those roles. It is not enough to select people in the organization who seem "right" for the job. Not only should the experience and duties be considered, but also the personality, the leadership skills, and the readiness for taking on a key leadership role.

Next, determine which members to consider for the leadership positions. It is best to identify this group with an objective system instead of just selecting "favorites." One option is for members to self-select into the process. This way, those who are already interested in the leadership roles will volunteer. They may be the most likely to take it seriously. Several "hopefuls" should be identified for each position to be filled. This allows the potential leaders to be "groomed," trained, and mentored for the possibility of filling the leadership positions. When the time comes for the position to be filled, there will be several people from which to choose, all of whom have had the time to develop for the new role.

At least one of them may be ready to meet the requirements. *In order to prepare potential leaders, the gap between what they are ready for now and what preparation they need to be ready for the job when it is available needs to be determined. This information can help determine what training, experience, and mentoring is needed.* By considering their past performance as a volunteer, past experience, fit with the organizational culture, and other members' acceptance of them as a potential leader, the best fit can be determined. Also, ensure that the potential leaders are willing to carry out the organization's mission and to continue the organization's philosophy and culture.

Once the potential leaders have been identified, a plan for each of them should be developed. Each potential leader should be assigned a mentor; this mentor should be the person whom they may replace. The mentor and the potential leader should form a teacher-student relationship. When issues arise that need problem solving or decision making, the leader should meet with the potential leader to ask how he or she would handle the situation. Allow the potential leaders time to "shadow" the leaders.

If possible, allow them to attend board meetings and participate in the decision making. This is a great way to see how they problem solve and interact. The leaders may even want to present the potential leaders with a problem and allow them to solve it as a group without any benefit of the leaders' input. See if the potential leaders would react in a way that is suitable or favorable. Also allow them to participate in goal-setting activities, such as strategic planning or budgeting. It is important to see them in action.

This process should not be a means for the leaders to choose the person most like them. Because a potential leader solves problems the same way as the leader does not make him or her the best candidate. The board may want to plan to conduct interviews with each candidate, assessing his or her abilities to make decisions, solve problems, behave appropriately in sensitive situations and lead those who will report to him or her. If appropriate, it is a good idea to allow direct reports to have some say in who will lead them. Finally, evaluate the succession planning efforts. What went well? What went wrong? What could be done differently? Make suggestions and recommendations for improving the process so that it runs more smoothly next time. If all goes as planned, the succession planning process will ensure a smooth transition and a new leader who is prepared for his or her role in the organization.

Succession Planning Process

The following steps should be followed: determine the key leaders for whom successors will be identified; identify the competencies of current key leaders; Identify experience and duties required; identify personality, political savvy, judgement; identify leadership skills; select the high-potential members who will participate in succession planning; identify gap between what the high-potential members are able to do presently and what they must do in the leadership role; create a development plan for each high-potential member to prepare him or her for the leadership position; perform development activities with each high-potential member; interview and select a member for the new leadership position and evaluate succession planning efforts and make changes to program based on evaluation for future programs.

Conclusion

I believe that after reading this book you have learned many things about how you can start and grow a successful great business that will help you achieve your dream and more importantly become a successful wealthy Entrepreneur. You have learned the secrets that will now make you one of the successful wealthy Entrepreneurs. Since you now know what it takes to become a successful wealthy Entrepreneur the next step is to learn how to apply all the information that you have learned from this book to your own personal situation.

This process will be the practical application and implementation of what you have learned in this book put into action in your own life. By that I mean, you need to make a decision on what you want to accomplish and determine the best way for you to accomplish that goal. Let me point out that the phenomenonto become a successful wealthy Entrepreneur is possible. Success is not a matter of luck or accident or being in the right place at the right time. Success is possible and by practicing what you have just learned, you will move to the front line in life and with no doubt you are relocating to the top as a champion in your own area and from today you will not scratch with turkeys but eagles.

You will have an edge over those who do not know or who do not practice these techniques and strategies. If you consistently do the things that other successful people do, nothing in this world will stop you from becoming a great success yourself. You are now the architect of your own destiny. You are behind the steering wheel of your own life. I wish you well and indeed when you become a successful wealthy Entrepreneur come and share me your wealth.

Lastly, your future is where you are going to take a big step of either starting a successful great business or even now if you are already involved in business,you are going to take everything that you have learned from this book to run your great business that will usher you into becoming a successful wealthy Entrepreneur the same way that millionaire or billionaire business owners or managers have always been running their businesses. I would like to encourage you to spot opportunities in the marketplace, learn how to develop opportunities that exist in the marketplace and you will be in charge of your destiny.

References

Books

Aaker, D.A. (2001), Strategic Market Managing, 6th ed. (New Jersey: John Wiley & Sons, Inc)

Aqualiano, N. (2001) Operations Management (New Jersey: McGraw – Hill Companies, Inc)

Bearden, L. (1990), 'Five Imperatives for improving service quality' (Great Brain: Ashford Colour Press)

Boyett, J. and Boyett, J. (1998), The Guru Guide (New Jersey: John Wiley & Sons, Inc)

Buswell, D. (1896), The development of quality measurement system for a UK Bank (London: Phillip Allan Oxford Press)

Blue's Clues for Success: The 8 Secrets Behind a Phenomenal Business by Diane Tracy (Dearborn, 2002).

Chandler, A. (1992) Strategy and Structure (Great Britain: MIT Press)

Charan, R. and Tichy, N. (1999), Every Business is Growth Business: How your Company Can prosper year after year (New Jersey: John Wiley and Sons, Inc)

Chase, R. (2004), Competitive Edge (New Jersey: McGraw – Hill Companies, Inc)

Church, G. (1999), Market Research: Methological Foundation, 7th ed. (London)

Cox, K. and Kotler P. (1998), Marketing Managing and Strategy: 4th ed. (New Jersey: Prentice Hall, Inc)

Cohen, D, and Prusak, L. (2001), "How to Invest in Social Capital" Haward Business Review Volume 79 no. 6 pp 86 – 95

Cole, G.A. (1997) Management Theory and Practice, (Great Britain: Ashford Colour Press, Gosport)

D,Aven R. (2002), "The Empire Strikes Back – Counter Revelatory Strategies for Industry Leaders" Harvard Business Review, Volume 80. no. 11, pp 69 – 79.

Daniels, J. (2004), International Business, (USA: Pearson Educational Limited)

David, F.R. (2001), Strategic Management – Concepts and Cases 8th ed. (New Jersey: Practice Hal, Inc)

Doyley, P. (2002) Marketing Management and Strategy, 3rd ed. (USA: Pearson

Education Limited)

Duck, J. (1993:109), Managing Change: The Art of Balancing, Harvard Business Review August

East, R. (1997), Consumer Behaviour: Advances, and Application in Marketing (London: Prentice Hall, Inc)

Ellis, G. (2007), Zero to Million: How to Build a Company to One Million Dollars in Sales (New Jersey: McGraw – Hill Companies, Inc)

Gerson, R. (1994), Measuring Customers Satisfaction (London: Kegan Kegan Limited)

Guerrilla Marketing: Secrets for Making Big Profits from Your Small Businessby Jay Conrad Levinson (Mariner Books, 1998).

Harrigan, K. and Porter, M. (1983), "End – Game Strategies for Declining Industries" Harvard Business Review, July August.

Hisrich, R. (1998) Entrepreneurship, (USA: McGraw – Hill Companies, Inc)

Jeffrey, G. (2001:175), Journal of Business Venture, Harvard Business Review, July

Jones, G. (2005) How to launch and grow the new business, (Great Britain: Bell & Bain Ltd)

Karakaya, F., (2002), "Barriers to Entry in Industrial Markets" Journal of Business and Industrial Marketing, Vol. 17 Issue 5

Lash, L.M. (1920), "Care in service Business" Business and finance Review, pp26 – 30

Laura, M. (1996), Building Adaptive Firm, Small Business Forum (Great Britain: Bell & Bain Lt)

McDonald, M. (1990), Marketing Plans: How to prepare them, How to use them, 4th ed (USA)

McConnell, C.R. and Brue, S.L. (2002). Economics (New Jersey: McGraw – Hill Companies, Inc)

McHugh, M. (2001), Understanding Business, (USA:McGraw – Hill Companies,Inc)

Melkam,A. (1979), How to Handle Major Customers Profitably (USA: Butter - Heinemann)

Nellis, J. (2004), Essence of Business Economics (India: Prentice Hall Private Limited)

Nickles, W. McHugh, J. et al (2005), Understanding Business (New York: McGraw – Hill Companies, Inc)

Oakland, J. (2001), Total Organizational Excellence – Achieving World – Class Performance (USA: Butterworth - Heinemann)

Olson, P. (1993), "Entrepreneurship Start – Up and growth" Business and Finance Review, pp 5 – 20

Own Your Own Corporation: Why the Rich Own Their Own Companies and Everyone Else Works for Them by Garrett Sutton, Robert T.

Pardo, C. (1999), "Key Account Management in Business – to – Business Field: A French Overview" Journal of Business and Industrial Marketing, Vol. 14 Issue 4

Peters, M. (1998), Entrepreneurship, (USA:McGraw – Hill Companies Inc)

Porters, M. (1979), "How Competitive Forces Shape Strategy" Harvard Business Review March – April.

Portraits of Success: 9 Keys to Sustaining Value in Any Business by James Olan Hutcheson (Dearborn, 2002).

Potter, D. (1999), "Success Under Fire: Policies to Prosper in Hostile Time" California Management review, Winter, PP 24 – 38

Radebaugh, L. (2002), International Business, (USA: McGraw Hill Companies,Inc)

Registrar of Companies Data Bank (2008)

Rigby, D. (2002), "Moving Upwards in Downturn" Harvard Business Review Vol. 80 no. 11,pp99-105

Robbins, S.P. (2001), Organizational Behaviour (New Jersey:Prentice Hall, Inc)

Resnblun P. (2003), "Bottom Feeding for Blockbuster Business" Harvard Business Review Volume 81 no. 3, pp52 – 59

OECD (2011), "Public support for business R&D", in OECD, Business Innovation Policies: Selected Country Comparisons, OECD Publishing.

OECD (2010), Why Is Administrative Simplification So Complicated? Looking Beyond 2010, Cutting Red Tape, OECD Publishing.

OECD (2010), SMEs, Entrepreneurship and Innovation, OECD Studies on SMEs and Entrepreneurship, OECD Publishing.

Saunders, M. Lewis P. et al (2000), Research Methods of Business Students, 2nd ed. (Great Britain: Ashford Colour Press Ltd)

Scarborough, M (2003), Effective Small Business, (USA: Pearson Education Limited)

Schumpeter, J. (1996), An Intrinsic Desire to Succeed, (USA: Pearson Education Limited)

Spencer, R. (1999), "Key Accounts: Effectively Managing Strategic Complexity" Journal of Business and Industrial Marketing, Vol 14 Issue 4

Stalk, G. Stern, C (1998), "Perspective on Strategy from the Boston Consulting Group" (USA: John Wiley and Sons, Inc)

Stevenson, W. (2005), Operations Management, (New York: McGraw – Hill Companies, Inc)

Sullivan, D. (2001), International Business, (USA: Pearson Education Limited)

Wilson, D. (1999), Organizational Marketing (New Jersey: International Thosmson Publishing)

World Bank (2013), Doing Business 2013: Smarter Regulations for Small and Medium-Size Enterprises, The World Bank Group, Washington, DC.

Young, E. (1993), "Entrepreneurship's Requisite Areas of Development: A Survey of Top Executives in Successful Entrepreneurial Firm" Journal of Business venture (March 1993)

Zimmer, T. (2000) An Entrepreneurial Approach, (USA: McGraw – Hill Companies,Inc)

Magazines and Newspapers

Black Enterprise <www.blackenterprise.com
Business 2.0 <www.business2.com
Business Startups <www.entrepreneur.com
Business Week <www.businessweek.com
Entrepreneur <www.entrepreneur.com
Fast Company www.fastcompany.com
Forbes <www.forbes.com
www.fortune.com
Franchise Handbook www.franchise1.com
Harvard Business Review <www.harvardbusinessonline.com
Inc. www.inc.com
Red Herring <www.redherring.com
Wall Street Journal<www.wsj.com

Other Web Sites

www.MrAllBiz.com
business.lycos.com
smallbusiness.yahoo.com
www.aarpsmallbiz.com
www.about.com/smallbusiness
www.asbdc-us.org
www.att.sbresources.com
www.bcentral.com
ww.bizland.com
www.bloomberg.com
www.business.gov
www.busop1.com
www.chamberbiz.com
www.entreworld.com
www.isquare.com
www.onlinewbc.gov
www.quicken.com/small_business
www.sba.gov
www.score.org
www.usatoday.com/money/smallbusiness/front.htm
www.winwomen.org
www.workz.com

Printed in the United States
by Baker & Taylor Publisher Services